BAR EXAM SURVIVAL

MICHAEL STOCKMAN, ESQ.

Wolters Kluwer
Law & Business

Published by Wolters Kluwer Law & Business in New York.

Wolters Kluwer Law & Business serves customers worldwide with CCH, Aspen Publishers, and Kluwer Law International products. (www.wolterskluwerlb.com)

Cover image licensed by Hunor Focze/Bigstock.com

To contact Customer Service, e-mail customer.service@wolterskluwer.com,
call 1-800-234-1660, fax 1-800-901-9075, or mail correspondence to:

Wolters Kluwer Law & Business
Attn: Order Department
PO Box 990
Frederick, MD 21705

Printed in the United States of America.

1 2 3 4 5 6 7 8 9 0

ISBN 978-1-4548-3772-5

About Wolters Kluwer Law & Business

Wolters Kluwer Law & Business is a leading global provider of intelligent information and digital solutions for legal and business professionals in key specialty areas, and respected educational resources for professors and law students. Wolters Kluwer Law & Business connects legal and business professionals as well as those in the education market with timely, specialized authoritative content and information-enabled solutions to support success through productivity, accuracy and mobility.

Serving customers worldwide, Wolters Kluwer Law & Business products include those under the Aspen Publishers, CCH, Kluwer Law International, Loislaw, ftwilliam.com and MediRegs family of products.

CCH products have been a trusted resource since 1913, and are highly regarded resources for legal, securities, antitrust and trade regulation, government contracting, banking, pension, payroll, employment and labor, and healthcare reimbursement and compliance professionals.

Aspen Publishers products provide essential information to attorneys, business professionals and law students. Written by preeminent authorities, the product line offers analytical and practical information in a range of specialty practice areas from securities law and intellectual property to mergers and acquisitions and pension/benefits. Aspen's trusted legal education resources provide professors and students with high-quality, up-to-date and effective resources for successful instruction and study in all areas of the law.

Kluwer Law International products provide the global business community with reliable international legal information in English. Legal practitioners, corporate counsel and business executives around the world rely on Kluwer Law journals, looseleafs, books, and electronic products for comprehensive information in many areas of international legal practice.

Loislaw is a comprehensive online legal research product providing legal content to law firm practitioners of various specializations. Loislaw provides attorneys with the ability to quickly and efficiently find the necessary legal information they need, when and where they need it, by facilitating access to primary law as well as state-specific law, records, forms and treatises.

ftwilliam.com offers employee benefits professionals the highest quality plan documents (retirement, welfare and non-qualified) and government forms (5500/PBGC, 1099 and IRS) software at highly competitive prices.

MediRegs products provide integrated health care compliance content and software solutions for professionals in healthcare, higher education and life sciences, including professionals in accounting, law and consulting.

Wolters Kluwer Law & Business, a division of Wolters Kluwer, is headquartered in New York. Wolters Kluwer is a market-leading global information services company focused on professionals.

About the Author

Michael Stockman, Esq. is a Phi Beta Kappa graduate of Harvard College and received his JD from Harvard Law School. He is a member of the Massachusetts and New York Bars.

Table of Contents

Preface

What I found most nerve-wracking about the bar was not knowing what to expect. I'd heard so much about it but still didn't know what it would be like.

I decided to write this book to give examinees a real taste of what the bar exam experience feels like, from the first day of bar prep through the exam days themselves.

I provide examples from my own experience taking the NY and MA bar exams in 2010 and 2011.

I also share strategies I devised to manage BarBri, the prep course I took twice. I explain the strategies that worked for me, from how to get organized to specific advice about condensing notes.

In addition, I offer you some practical advice about the test days themselves. Things I hadn't thought of and that you might not either.

Finally, there's some advice about how to manage the stress and anxiety of bar prep and the exam.

What This Guide Is

- a description of what the experience of taking the bar exam is really like

- study tips, including how to best manage BarBri
- advice on how to manage stress and anxiety
- practical advice, such as what to bring to test day

What This Guide Is Not

- substantive legal review
- how to crack the MBE
- a collection of sample questions

Chapter 1: About This Guide

Before we begin, I'd like to point out a few things about this book and its author.

Who Are You Again?

I've never taught bar prep, I don't work for BarBri, and I don't teach at a law school.

I've always been a good student and test-taker, and recently taking two bar exams gave me some strong insights about the best way to navigate the process.

Bar Prep At Your Law School?

Increasing numbers of law schools now require bar prep classes during 3L year. If you were fortunate enough to take one of those, you're most likely ahead of the game. Bear with me as I introduce elements and components of the bar with which you may already be familiar.

Informed Consent

While meant to be universally applied, some of the advice in this book may not work for you. For example, I don't recommend too much time spent prepping for the MultiState Performance Test, should your jurisdiction offer this component. Perhaps you feel differently and want to spend more study time on it. That's great—I encourage you to modify or dismiss outright any pieces of advice that don't work for you.

BarBri Mania

I took BarBri twice. It's the most popular prep course, and one chapter (Chapter 4) refers to its components specifically as I offer advice on how to manage the overwhelming scope of the course itself. If you're not taking BarBri, some of the advice may still apply to your bar course or solo prep. If you aren't in BarBri, don't worry about the unfamiliar names of the various BarBri components. These are the same types of materials all examinees will be dealing with in one form or another.

Jurisdiction Constriction

This is a general guide that doesn't address the specifics of any state's exam. I do use examples from my experience prepping for the NY and MA bar exams but also address the exam components common to all jurisdictions. For more specific information about each jurisdiction, please visit the website of the National Conference of Bar Examiners at www.ncbex.org.

Chapter 2: Myths And Realities

The Bar Exam holds a unique place in the popular mythology surrounding the legal profession. Lawyers and non-lawyers alike inflate what is basically a two or three day professional licensing test into the Mother Of All Examinations, a hot sweaty summer ritual of intellectual torment which mysteriously transforms law students into lawyers.

I'd like to start, then, by confronting some of the myths that you'll encounter as you begin your preparation for the bar exam.

Myth: This Is Going To Be The Worst Summer (Winter) Of My Life

While you will most likely not confuse the eight to ten weeks you spend preparing for the bar exam with a tropical paradise, this does not have to be the worst summer, or for February examinees, winter, of your life.

The principal tool for achieving this is to do your best to maintain a calm observational standpoint on the larger process of bar exam prep and examination. I'll discuss ways to do this in Chapter Five, Maintaining Psychological Sovereignty.

Myth: I'm Not Good At Standardized Tests, So The Bar Exam Is Going To Be Particularly Hard For Me

Not true. The difference between most American standardized testing and the bar exam is that the former do not pull from a pre-announced body of knowledge as the bar exam does. Instead of the brain teasers on the math or verbal portions of the SAT's, most aspects of the bar exam on both the essay and multistate days involve finding the law you know and making quick guesses on the law you don't.

Practicing real released or prep course prepared simulated questions will help you improve your bar exam score. Undoubtedly, there will be a few out-there zingers on both the morning and afternoon sections of the Multistate Bar Exam—just make quick guesses and move on, as these are likely some of the 10 experimental questions that are not scored.

When it comes to the MBE, I encourage you to keep in the forefront of your mind that in order to pass in most jurisdictions—and assuming an average performance on the other day(s) of the exam—you need to get around 130 questions right. Since there are 200 questions, 100 in each three hour session, that means that you could record the answer "A" for the first 70 questions in a row, without reading them, and still be able to pass the exam.

I'm not recommending you do this, of course. I bring it up to stress the importance of not getting bogged down on any one question. Just make your best guess, record an answer on your answer sheet and circle the question in your test booklet to return to if you finish with time to spare.

Be prepared for rough patches. Sometimes the MBE will hit you with three, four, even five long, complicated mortgage-type questions in a row. It's perfectly understandable that this would rattle even the most confident examinee. Don't let a false belief about your supposed poor standardized test performance lead you to experience these patches as somehow corroborative of your supposed test-taking deficiencies. For more on the MBE, please see Chapter 9, Daily Work.

Myth: I'm Too Old To Take The Bar Exam

I took the Mass Bar at 37 and the NY Bar at 38. A surprising number of my fellow examinees were ten, twenty, even thirty years older than I.

I think being older is more of a benefit than a detriment to preparing for the bar. By virtue of being older, you'll be more careful, more attentive, and detail-oriented. In fact, you may well annoy the younger students around you with your earnest questions about what exactly the

BarBri lecturer meant about short-term leases and the Statute of Frauds.

Being older means being wiser, and having more experience with the normal ups and downs of life, which means having more tolerance for the ambiguities, stresses, and frustrations of bar exam preparation.

I'm not promising or recommending a prep period free of anxiety and frustration. And there can be some initial challenges for the older student, such as the higher likelihood of family and professional responsibilities competing for time or a long period between graduation from law school and the bar exam.

Overall, though, I encourage any qualified person to take the bar, no matter what their age. For more on being an older test taker, please see Chapter 7, For Older Examinees And Those Returning After Time Away From The Law.

Myth: I'm From A Foreign Country: I'll Never Pass The Bar Exam

At my swearing-in ceremony in Albany in June of 2011, I was happily surprised by the number of foreign candidates being inducted into the New York Bar.

They were from over thirty countries, and a few I talked to spoke good-naturedly about their multiple attempts to pass the exam and their ultimate success.

They passed and so can you.

For more advice for foreign students, please see Chapter 6, For Test Takers Born Or Trained Abroad.

Myth: February Is Easier Than July

In many jurisdictions the passage rate for February examinees is substantially lower than for their July counterparts.

This leads some to believe that the February administration of the bar exam is "easier" to pass. The logic here is that most unsuccessful summer candidates will repeat the exam in February and these repeat takers are less fierce competition than first-time test takers.

Others believe the February administration is harder to pass. This camp sites the lower passage rate and maintains that most repeat takers will have an advantage because they've already experienced the bar exam and know what to expect.

I think both points of view are irrelevant. The scaling of the exam attempts to even out differences in difficulty from one administration of the exam to the next.

That's not to say there aren't qualitative differences in taking the bar exam during summer as opposed to winter. If you live in a place with clearly defined seasons, studying and attending class during sweltering summer days is quite different from reading your Contracts outline as snow falls peacefully outside your window.

Due to the greater number of people who take the July administration, the summer exam experience is more social. If you take BarBri or a similar prep course, you'll be reminded of the group experience of college or law school.

Winter is more low-key and self-directed.

My advice is to take the bar exam administration that makes you most comfortable. If you're a summer-loving volleyball player with season tickets to the Red Sox, you might find it less painful to study during the dreary winter.

Alternatively, if winter tends to slow you down or depress you, maybe summer is better for you.

I took the MA bar in July, and the NY bar in February. Although I found it easier to study during a brutal winter, I missed some of the companionship and camaraderie I found during the summer experience.

In sum, if you find yourself fortunate enough to be able to choose between a winter or summer administration, use personal criteria and not pseudo-statistical analyses of passage rates.

Chapter 3: Bar Review Courses And Taking Take Two Bar Exams At Once

Just Do It

The vast majority of bar examinees take one of a handful of commercial bar prep courses. You've most likely heard of or are already enrolled in BarBri, by far the largest. Others include Kaplan/PMBR, BarMax, and AmeriBar. In addition, private bar exam tutors offer their expertise in every jurisdiction, and subscription websites—not courses in themselves but helpful complements—are becoming more popular, such as Separac.com for NY Bar test takers.

(Separac.com also has a great deal of free content on the NY bar that I encourage all test takers to check out.)

Bar prep courses cost several thousand dollars. BarBri, for example, charges nearly $4,000 for its New York course.

The expense of the bar course may tempt some examinees to forgo one. The rationalizations begin:

- I'm a JD—a *Doctor* of the *Law*—what do I need with recorded lectures?
- A friend of mine who took the bar last year gave me her books and notes so I'll just use those.

- Did you say 4K? Sweet, I'll study on my own, pay down my law school debt, and get a new flat screen.

Understandable thoughts all, but don't give in. Why?

Doing fill-in-the-blank outlines while watching recorded lectures may seem an activity more suited for advanced apes than future human attorneys.

But what this activity achieves is a mild form of brainwashing or hypnotism. As the professors rattle off the black letter and you fill in the blanks, your mind starts to absorb the material. This serves as a base track that is repeatedly reinforced as you condense your notes and then review and memorize them.

Another good reason for taking a prep course is that the designers of the course select, brief, and emphasize the most relevant law. The Bar Examiners of each state release exhaustive lists of the legal content that may be tested as part of the bar exam. Attempting to tackle this content yourself and assembling the relevant materials could take a very long time—time better spent studying. It probably wouldn't be the most thrilling task either.

When you enroll in a bar prep course, everything except actual studying is done for you.

For most, this makes the bar prep experience more manageable.

Throughout this guide, I will emphasize the importance of maintaining psychological sovereignty throughout the experience, particularly in Chapter Three. I think this is easiest done in the context of a larger external structure such as that provided by bar prep courses.

One Is More Than Enough

One bar review course is not only adequate, but by mid-July or February it will seem like too much.

Some believe that the best approach is to take two courses—one, such as BarBri, for the black letter and essay prep, and another, such as PMBR, for MBE prep.

I think this is overkill for most examinees. At the beginning of the bar exam preparation experience, it's perfectly understandable that anxiety about the unknown would lead you to believe that the more courses in which you enroll, the better prepared you will ultimately be.

But I think this strategy often backfires. It's hard enough—and perhaps even unadvisable (see below)—to keep up with one course. If you're taking two or more, it's inevitable that you will start to fall behind, and this will create more unnecessary anxiety.

Furthermore, most people fare rather dismally on the first sets of practice questions they attempt. This is normal and to be expected, but it can be unsettling. Multiplying this experience by more than one course would be even more unsettling, creating even more unnecessary stress.

Do the best you can to resist the tug to purchase more than one course. Remember, you can always add another course a few weeks into the studying process if you feel it's necessary.

Brick & Mortar Location or OnLine Streaming?

BarBri and most other bar prep courses offer several different methods of accessing lecture materials. Traditionally, there were live lectures in select locations and videotaped presentations of these lectures at satellite locations. This remains the case, except for the small shift from videotapes to DVD's.

The last few years have seen the advent of the option of watching the lectures online via streaming video on demand.

Some maintain that it's best to attend either the live or video lectures on a consistent basis and use the streaming lectures solely for make-ups. I think the logic behind this viewpoint is that if you're disciplined and travel to the live/video location every day you are less likely to fall behind. Some may have difficulty concentrating on the streaming lectures at home amidst the temptations of Comedy Central, refrigerator, and bed.

I tried both approaches. When I took BarBri for the Massachusetts bar, I attended every 6pm DVD lecture at Boston College Law School.

When I took BarBri for the NY Bar, I attended every 9am DVD lecture at the BarBri offices on St. James Street in downtown Boston until a blizzard led to the cancellation of two days of class. Streaming the lectures online from

BarBri's website during those snow days was so convenient that I never went back to the brick and mortar location.

There were many things I liked about video streaming. First, I actually found it easier to concentrate at home. I connected headphones to my iMac and played the videos in full screen. Gone were the distractions of some of the noisier members of the BarBri classroom—one student in particular drove me nuts every day by chomping away on an apple.

Second, on some days I blew through more than one day's worth of lectures, freeing up patches of extra days to spend condensing my notes and start memorizing. I did discover that I had a limit. Watching two day's worth of lectures in one day was fine. But slogging through three days of online lectures became exhausting, particularly if they were the longer ones which lasted around 4 hours each.

Third, I could pick and choose which lecture topics to watch in which order. Liberated from the BarBri schedule, I could watch Evidence weeks before or after it was presented on the in-class DVD presentations. There is one limitation. When BarBri films new live lectures for your course, there can be a delay of several days before they are posted on the site.

There were a few things that left me unfulfilled about watching the lectures online at home. I did not have the benefit of a community of fellow examinees. Even though I found some of my peers a tad irritating, such as the apple muncher, it was nice to be in the environment of other people undergoing bar prep. This was especially true the first time I took BarBri. The 6pm BC Law crew was small and friendly, and that helped.

That said, the second time around I knew more about what to expect during the process and to some extent enjoyed being more self-directed and watching more of the lectures at home.

I imagine that some students got together in groups to watch the streaming lectures at home together. It seems to me that this could be an enjoyable way to arrange things, especially if someone has a projector or flat screen that can be hooked up to a computer and display the videos in a large format. Popcorn, anyone?

I encourage everyone enrolled in a prep course that offers on-demand streaming video to experiment with both the online and real-world approaches until you find the right mix for you.

Live Or Video?

If you've decided that streaming videos at home is not for you, you still have the further choice of attending either live lectures or a video location.

One benefit of the live locations is that they begin—and end—a week or more before the video locations. While few if any are in a great rush to begin their bar prep course, the extra week or more between the end of the lectures and the examination itself can be extremely helpful, as this is when most examinees pull everything together. For more on this crucial period, please see Chapter Ten, The Last Two Weeks, and Chapter Eleven, The Last 100 Hours.

Are You A Morning Or An Evening Person?

If you choose to attend a video location, the final choice you have is whether to attend a morning or night session.

I suspect that this mostly depends upon your schedule. If you are working while studying for the bar, most likely the night schedule is better for you (unless you're a bartender, DJ, or security guard).

If you are devoting yourself full time to studying and can choose any time, I would ask yourself a few simple questions.

First, are you a morning person or a night person?

Second, ask yourself which of the following two scenarios is more appealing to you. If you attend class in the morning, you'll be getting up early, going to class, having lunch, and studying in the afternoon and evening. If you attend class at night, you'll be returning from class relatively late (usually after 10pm), and most likely sleeping in a bit and then studying during the morning and afternoon.

Choose the one that you believe fits you better.

In my experience, the morning classes are substantially more crowded than the evening ones. (The live morning locations tend to be the most crowded of all and are the very first to fill up.) The evening attendees also tend to be older, as they are often occupied with work and or family obligations during the day.

Double Trouble?

One final choice for certain examinees is whether to take two bar exams in one administration. Certain jurisdictions stagger the date of their local day examination(s) to make this feasible. For example, the NY bar's local day is always on a Tuesday, and the MA bar always on a Thursday. The MBE, in all jurisdictions, is scheduled on Wednesdays.

This permits you to take both the MA and NY bar exams in a single administration. It does, however, require a good bit of traveling at a rather stressful time. You'd sit in New York for the local day on Tuesday, and then, at your option, sit for the MBE in either New York or Mass on

Wednesday, and finish up in Mass with the MA local day on Thursday.

Most bar prep courses encourage you to enroll in the course for the more difficult state and then issue you secondary materials for the second jurisdiction. In the above scenario, then, you would enroll in the NY course and then pick up books on MA local law to review on your own.

A recent change in certain jurisdictions increases the appeal of the strategy of taking two bar exams at once. Until recently, some jurisdictions such as New York would allow examinees who'd taken the MBE in any state in the immediately preceding administration of the exam to use this score instead of having to re-take the MBE.

Unfortunately, this is no longer allowed. Now examinees must take the MBE again, even if they took it in the immediately preceding administration.

Is this enough of a reason to take two bar exams at once? Before making this decision, there are a few other aspects of the multi-bar experience to explore.

First, determine if being a member of the second state's bar association would truly be useful for you. Multiple bar admissions mean multiple dues and sometimes multiple CLE requirements.

Second, determine if you need to be a member of the second jurisdiction right away. Many jurisdictions offer Admission On Motion after you've practiced in another jurisdiction for a number of years. This is a wonderfully painless way to become a member of another jurisdiction's bar that requires no bar exam.

Third, try a thought experiment in which you imagine what it would be like to experience at least three exam days in two different jurisdictions. Could you psychologically prepare yourself so it wouldn't be too overwhelming to, say, leave Albany at 6pm after the Wednesday administration of the Multistate and make the three and a half hour drive over to Boston, arriving late at night and managing to make it to the Harbor Convention Center by 8am the following morning?

If you have classmates who are also interested in taking two bar exams, coordinating travel plans with them can cut down costs and add some camaraderie.

Chapter 4: BarBri-Specific Advice

Since more than a majority of bar examinees take BarBri—and since I myself took BarBri twice, once for Massachusetts and once for New York—I'd like to offer some BarBri-specific advice. If you've chosen not to take BarBri, much of the information in this section is applicable to other courses, as well as to aspects of self-study.

Apologies To Mr. Conviser And The Big Bastards

Upon your enrollment in BarBri, you'll be the proud recipient of two heavy cardboard boxes of books. These new additions to your library will include two enormous, encyclopedic tomes, one detailing the six Multistate subjects—Evidence, Constitutional Law, Criminal Law and Procedure, Torts, and Property—and the other the local topics covered by the jurisdiction for which you're sitting. I refer to these as the Big Bastards. Another volume will include local essay questions and answers, and, if your jurisdiction offers it, yet another volume will contain practice Multistate Performance Test questions. Finally, there will be the famous Conviser Mini Review Volume, which digests both the Multistate and local law in condensed outlines with charts and diagrams.

BarBri recommends you read the Conviser Mini Review for each topic prior to the lectures covering that topic. They also recommend that you read the detailed outline for subjects you never took in law school or with which you are struggling.

I experimented with reading everything (both the larger outline and Conviser); reading just Conviser; and reading nothing.

What I found was that there was little benefit to reading the detailed outline. There was simply too much information to process, and by the final week before the exam I recalled almost nothing of what I'd read in the big outline. Furthermore, reading the detailed outline is quite time-consuming, and I think this time is better spent attending and/or making up all lectures and condensing notes.

The Conviser outline was slightly more helpful. First, I recommend tearing apart Mr. Conviser. Literally. I tore out each subject, stapled the pages together, and then further secured one of the sides with masking tape. This resulted in my having short, Conviser pamphlets for each subject I carried with me to review at odd moments such as when on the subway or when walking the dog.

Conviser is also helpful for its wonderful chart summaries of important legal principles. These are particularly helpful for visual learners.

Most surprisingly, the most helpful reading schedule for me personally was not to read any of the BarBri books at all. Occasionally I looked up a topic or sub-topic in Conviser or one of the Big Bastards, but overall I used the lecture handouts and my condensed lecture notes as the Holy Grail of my studying.

This requires having a certain amount of blind faith in BarBri and the material selected for lecture by the BarBri lecturers. Since I ended up passing both exams, I feel this faith was ultimately well-placed.

But as with all of my advice, I encourage you to experiment on your own and discover what works best with your individual learning style.

Relating To BarBri Lecturers

In psychoanalytic theory, the concept of transference refers to the relationship between the patient and the analyst. As part of the process of integrating one's past conflicts, they are re-lived as the patient transfers or projects onto the analyst important roles from childhood—Mother, Father, etc.

What does this have to do with studying for the bar exam?

Both times I took BarBri, I found that I had surprisingly strong reactions—both positive and negative—to various lecturers.

When I had strong positive reactions—as I did, say, to Robert Schechter for Torts and Family Law or Richard Freer for Corporations and MA Procedure—sitting through the lectures was almost enjoyable. I also found it easier to recall some snippets of the lectures while working through the practice questions and even on the exam days themselves.

Due to the nature of my personality I enjoyed their use of deadpan humor and the way they presented the material.

When I had strong negative reactions to a BarBri Professor, sitting through two, three, or more days of lecture was incredibly painful.

What was fascinating was that my BarBri classmates often loved professors I found annoying and disliked professors I loved. This illuminated for me the overall subjectivity and transference-like nature of the experience.

My advice is to allow yourself to have these experiences of attraction and repulsion to BarBri lecturers and adjust accordingly. It's a wonderful thing when a legal topic you fear and or dislike is presented by a lecturer you love. Suddenly, the topic is transformed into something a lot more manageable.

When you encounter a lecturer who just isn't your kind of person, I'd advise you to hang in there and endure all of their lectures. If your dislike is based upon the lecturer's disorganized or confusing approach—and some BarBri professors are much better organized than others—do your best to make it through the lectures and then turn to Conviser or one of the Big Bastards to clarify the overall organization of the topic.

The Paced Program Is A Hysterical Compulsive

The centerpiece of BarBri is the Paced Program. This is a day by day schedule of reading assignments, practice MBE questions, practice essay questions, and online workshops. It is available in both hard copy and online at the BarBri website.

Both times I took BarBri, I didn't come close to keeping up with the Paced Program. Most of my classmates didn't either.

I wished I had known this going in, because I found it nerve-wracking to start a course and, within a matter of days, find myself falling terribly behind.

I also feel that in my many attempts to catch up, I often wasted time doing Paced Program assignments when I should have been doing other things, such as condensing my notes, which were of a much higher priority level.

My second time through BarBri, I started to view the Paced Program as a neurotic. "Don't forget to spend three hours after lecture reviewing your notes!" it shrieked, "and then do three sets of practice questions, and then watch the two hour Multistate workshop for that topic online, and then do these five essays, and then and then and then!!!!"

I suspect it's nearly impossible to follow the Paced Program if you do the assignments with any kind of thoroughness or care.

That's why I recommend tailoring the Paced Program to your needs. Most importantly, when you begin to fall behind, don't freak out. You're not alone. Instead of trying to make-up the assignments you missed, continue along with the program as it suits you so you don't fall even further behind.

So how much of the Paced Program should you complete? I think this differs from person to person. As you go through week after week of BarBri, monitor yourself. What subjects are giving you the most difficulty? Do you struggle more with the practice essays, or with the practice multistate questions? Assess your strengths and weaknesses as objectively as possible and edit, modify, and abridge the Paced Program with them in mind.

Chapter 5: Maintaining Psychological Sovereignty

If there is a secret to the bar exam, it is this: The test is less one of innate legal knowledge or ability than one of managing the psychological stresses involved with organizing and becoming familiar with tremendous amounts of detailed information.

Sure, there are intellectual challenges involved with the bar exam. There are riddles like the Statute of Frauds and the brain teaser quality to decoding Future Interests or untangling hearsay within hearsay.

But the vast majority of concepts are straightforward.

The real test is more psychological than intellectual. It requires you to devise strategies to keep yourself from succumbing to the pressures you'll face during an intense period of study before two or more extensive days of testing.

In other words, you've got to find ways to stay on top of things and maintain psychological sovereignty over the experience.

What follows are specific strategies for achieving this.

The Bar Exam, The Movie, Starring YOU!

The bar exam is an inherently dramatic moment in a lawyer's career, a plot point in the larger story arc of a life in the law. After three years of law school, the bar exam is a threshold whose successful crossing transforms the JD holder into an authorized practitioner.

Dramatic doesn't have to mean frightening. Dramatic can also mean suspenseful, passionate, and cathartic.

One great, dorky way to insulate yourself from the waves of anxiety and helplessness that can be part of the bar exam experience is to think of yourself as the hero of a summer blockbuster movie in which a new law school graduate battles the bar exam preparation and examination process and is ultimately, wildly, successful.

Cast yourself in the genre of movie you most enjoy.

Since the bar exam involves a Rocky-esque period of training followed by two game days, athletic themes work well.

So do man or woman-against-the-system plots.

The possibilities are endless. Like Star Wars? Are you Yoda, aspiring Esquire? Prefer Nancy Drew? Lady Gaga Rocks The Bar? Or are you more of a cynical wiseacre—Tosh.O Skewers The Bar?

Emergency Vacations

If you find yourself feeling depleted, do yourself a favor and take an Emergency Vacation. Studying for the bar exam is like entering a long dark tunnel. The further in you get, the harder it is to see the light at either end and gauge where you've been and where you're going. Emergency Vacations can be as short as a one hour trip to an ice cream store and a walk in the park, to a three hour movie with a giant tub of popcorn, to a weekend away in the Hamptons, Cape Cod, Atlantic City, or other restful or amusing destination near you.

How do you know if you need an Emergency Vacation? Here's a symptom checklist:

- You try to study but your mind wanders
- You are falling asleep as you study
- You try to study but panic intervenes
- Just the sight of the BarBri materials on your desk makes you want to vomit

If you meet two or more of these criteria, it's time for an Emergency Vacation.

Here are some additional suggestions for Emergency Vacations:

- a nap (especially refreshing after a morning of BarBri lecture before beginning studying for the day)

- a run or other physical activity you enjoy that will temporarily drum the black letter out of your brain
- if you are single, a date with a new person—strut your bar exam mojo or strive for pity points
- painting, creative writing, photography, sculpting—engage in an art form that interests and relaxes you, allowing you to utilize that part of your brain the bar exam ignores
- a night of pub crawling with non-lawyer non-bar examining friends
- read a novel, either a legal thriller by fellow bar exam survivor John Grisham, or, for the

brave, haven't you been meaning to give Joyce's *Ulysses* another try?

If you don't have time for any of the above Emergency Vacations, you can also take a quick ten or fifteen minute break and engage in one of the following two types of thought experiments to center yourself.

Thought Experiment 1: Being A Lawyer Is A Beautiful Thing

Despite society's tendency to scapegoat lawyers, society's problem-solvers, for society's problems, practicing law is a wonderful thing. It is the practice of law that brought advancements in Civil Rights, has encouraged corporate responsibility, and permits those harmed who have little or no resources to obtain justice from powerful interests.

As you most likely have come to realize, the Bar Exam is not a wonderful thing. There's not much sense to it, and the correlation between it and either law school or the practice of law—the two things it should rationally reflect—are unclear at best. Also, the architecture of the exam and test prep courses encourage anxiety.

When studying for the bar exam has you anxious, frustrated, and exhausted, take an emergency moral vacation and contemplate what a wonderful profession you're about to join. Appreciate the power you're on the verge of being granted by society and the awesome responsibility accompanying it. How do you want to change the world?

Take that, Rule Against Perpetuities!

Thought Experiment 2: The Cosmological Perspective

A few weeks into your bar exam preparation, you will find the horizon of your life narrowing. You will be initiated into the cult of BarBri (or whatever prep course you choose to take), and daily attend three to four hour brainwashing sessions (the lectures), while clutching your sacred texts (Conviser and the Big Bastards). Your brain will feed upon a daily diet of law, law, and more law, and you will find it more and more difficult to communicate with "normal" people who are not studying for the bar exam. Your brain will struggle through a thicket of mnemonics, abbreviations, rules, principles, and criteria. The days will blur together.

At times like this, I recommend a thought experiment I call the Cosmological Perspective.

It's simple to perform. Go outside on a clear night, preferably in a place that's private and tranquil.

Look up at the stars.

Contemplate the enormity of the cosmos.

Think of how infinitesimal our little home planet Earth is in this context.

What does the Universe care about the Defeasible Fees?

Where in the Milky Way is there anxiety about the duties owed by property owners to known trespassers?

Is there life on Mars? If so, how anxious do you think the Martian community is about the hearsay exceptions?

Let your mind zoom out to the Big Picture.

What is the Bar Exam?

It's a test to get a license.

Were you this anxious about the test you took to get your driver's license?

Don't Drink The Kool-Aid

In order not to drink the Kool-Aid, you must first identify what the Kool-Aid is.

In the context of the bar exam preparation and examination experience, the Kool-Aid is the belief system that encourages the myths that the bar exam is impossible and that this is going to be the worst summer/winter of your life. These sorts of false beliefs often become self-fulfilling prophecies.

What's interesting is that some bar examinees seem to yearn for the bar exam process to fulfill their darkest and most anxious fantasies. You are probably familiar with this type from law school. These were the classmates who endlessly discussed the grading curves of 1L classes or who drove themselves crazy studying rarely-tested minutiae before exams. These were the students who seemed almost addicted to anxiety and wanted law school to reflect exaggerated cinematic and literary portrayals such as Scott Turow's *1L* or the 1980's movie *The Paper Chase*.

Take my advice above and script yourself into your own movie.

And when the Kool-Aid is passed around, take a pass and drink the cool clean water of psychological independence.

Don't Listen To Anyone Else

Again, I must emphasize this: Don't fall into the trap of letting the nervous people freaking out about the exam influence you.

A brief anecdote. During one of my BarBri classes, I found myself intimidated by two students who would talk loudly about their scores on the assigned sets of practice questions as the rest of us sat in silence waiting for the DVD lecture to begin.

On my first few BarBri practice MBE question sets, I was routinely getting as many as 18 out of 20 wrong. I was okay with this, because I knew that it'd been a while since law school and I hadn't started studying in earnest yet.

But listening to these conversations every day before lecture started to get me to doubt myself.

"I only got 15 out of 20 right on that first Property set," one of them would say.

"I got 18 right," the other would reply.

I wanted to start vomiting right there and then.

These students didn't limit their loud conversation to broadcasting their practice test scores. They discussed passage rates for the exam, the relative probability of the most difficult topics appearing on the local essay day, when the exam results would be announced, where the swearing-in ceremony would be, when it would be, what the law license would look like, and on and on and on.

After a while, I started arriving just moments before the DVD's started to avoid sitting through these unendurable dialogs.

About a month into the course, overhearing a conversation during one of the ten minute lecture breaks, I learned an amazing fact about these two students: They'd failed the previous administration of the bar exam!

This experience led me to an important conclusion about the bar exam—and maybe about life in general. Often those talking the most loudly and with the most apparent authority not only don't know what they are talking about, part of the reason they resort to such loud volume and posturing is to compensate for their insecurities.

So again, I beseech you: Don't listen to anyone else. I know that it's hard, but do your best to maintain ownership of your bar exam experience.

Time To Get Shrunk?

If you are already in counseling or analysis, you will find your therapist and sessions invaluably helpful during your bar exam adventure. Most therapists excel at helping those they counsel put anxiety-provoking experiences such as the bar exam into a larger context.

If you are not currently in therapy or have never tried any form of counseling, is this a good time to start?

It is a well-known psychiatric principle that periods of great stress and emotional strain can activate underlying mental, emotional, and spiritual complexes.

The bar exam can certainly be a period of great stress and strain.

As the weeks go by, if you find yourself feeling depressed, or if normal bar exam anxiety (i.e., "Holy crap I'm gonna fail!" feelings) intensifies into overwhelming anxiety (repeated bouts of insomnia, frequent vomiting, acid reflux and other gastro-intestinal travails, thoughts of self-harm), I'd advise you to get some help.

If you've never received counseling, you may be surprised by how much it can help you not only to reclaim yourself during the bar exam process, but also prove useful in navigating your life. Especially as you prepare to enter the legal profession, spending some time thinking through what you want from your life and your work could really pay dividends in the form of continuing life happiness.

If you're skeptical about therapy or feel it's not for you, there are many other options that fulfill the same function. Religious counseling, in the form of a church or madrasa group or meeting with your rabbi, can offer comfort as you progress through the bar exam. So can groups that you already may belong to, such as a book club, movie group, or AA.

What's important is not the form of the help you get, but that you identify as early as possible in the bar exam process that you need support and act accordingly.

Try To Enjoy The Adventure

In sum, the bar exam experience is an adventure—an adventure into the law, an adventure into studying, an adventure into your character and psyche and how you respond to stress.

While obviously not all aspects of the bar exam are enjoyable, try at least to relish the adventure from time to time.

Chances are very good that this will be the first and last time you ever prep for the bar exam. (And if not, well then the second time will be its own kind of adventure, with other insights and challenges. For more on that, please see Chapter 14, If You Need To Take It Again.)

Being a lawyer permits you a privilege few other professions offer: to advise and represent people and be trusted with their private, confidential struggles.

Enjoying this privilege and being a lawyer is the life adventure you have chosen for yourself. You were attracted to this work for a variety of reasons, some of which you know, and others which may reveal themselves as your career progresses.

Live this adventure robustly and on your own terms. Celebrate your individuality. And start now, with the bar exam preparation process.

Chapter 6: For Test Takers Born Or Trained Abroad

The bar exam is a difficult process for the American JD's who sit for it. Most of these examinees grew up in America speaking English, familiar with the larger outlines of the American political and legal system.

That you have decided to go up against not only the jurisdiction-specific day but also the MBE is impressive.

Why Take The Bar In A U.S. Jurisdiction?

Since you're reading this guide, chances are you've already decided to take a bar exam in an American jurisdiction.

But if you're not quite sure yet, here are some of the most common reasons lawyers born or trained overseas take a U.S. bar. Some have no choice in the matter. Either they work at foreign offices of U.S. firms which require U.S. bar passage for all lawyers, or are transferring or starting at a U.S. law firm and therefore need to get licensed. Other international lawyers take a U.S. bar to keep their employment options as globally flexible as possible. Still others take it for the added prestige U.S. bar membership adds to their practice in their home country, particularly for those seeking to represent American nationals in foreign legal matters.

It's Not Just Another Legal System, It's An Entirely Different Culture

A legal system is an abstraction when divorced from its cultural context.

There are three main areas where you'll want to educate yourself in order to best understand the larger structure of the American legal system:

1. The basic narrative history of the United States

The American legal system is best understood as part of the historical narrative of the United States. The good news is that since the United States is a relatively young country, many of these histories aren't that long. You can also search the web for histories in your native tongue.

2. The structure of American legal education

I think it would also be helpful to learn a bit about the structure of legal education in the United States. This is easily done by visiting American law schools on the internet, conversing with any American JD's you may know or meet during the process of bar prep, and scanning some of the study materials aimed at JD's on Amazon.com.

Not only will such familiarity help you understand some of the background references made by prep materials and lecturers, it will also give you a clear sense of the academic experiences of the majority of your fellow test-takers.

3. Contemporary American culture

Increasing your knowledge of contemporary American culture will help you out on the bar in a couple of ways. First, knowing a bit about current life in the United States will give you a background to the narratives in the essay questions, MBE, and MPT. Second, since legal dramas are popular in America, you can start to understand the various roles of the different players in the American legal system. This is particularly helpful if you were born or trained in a country without a common law system.

This can be the fun part of bar prep. Watch season after season of *Law and Order* without guilt as you become familiar with the American legal scene. Rent or download movies like *The Firm* or *A Civil Action* to view longer fictional portrayals of various aspects of American lawyering. Read books, in English or translation, such as Turrow's *Presumed Innocent* or Grisham's *The King of Torts*.

Keep in mind, of course, that these are fictional and therefore highly dramatized and stylized representations of the American legal profession. Do not reference them as authorities on the bar exam! Their best value lies in acclimating you to a big picture perspective of the United States and our legal system.

Befriend JD's

I'd also recommend that you befriend some American JD test takers. They are a great resource for any practical information, either about the American legal system or specifics such as hotel bookings, examination policies, and deadlines for various pieces of the Bar Exam application.

Language Games

An enormous hurdle faced by those raised or trained abroad in non-English speaking nations is language. Language is central to almost every aspect of the bar exam. The difference between a right and wrong answer on a MBE question often hinges on a sharp reading of the details of the question itself. And of course writing legal essays in English under extreme time pressure requires some degree of comfort with not just American English, but legal American English.

To address these difficulties, there are a new crop of online legal English training sites. The most popular of these, translegal.com, is a pay-site that specializes in training non-native English speakers in English legal terminology.

Other alternatives include joining an English-speaker's club in your home country (locate such a group on Facebook or Yahoo Groups), reading some materials aimed at first year (i.e. "1L") American JD's who are prepping for their first year exams in Contracts, Torts, Criminal Law, Civil Procedure, and Con Law, and exposing yourself to American culture in the form of television and movies, as discussed above.

Tailored Strategy?

Some overseas-trained lawyers devise study strategies around their discomfort with English.

One approach some students take is to focus heavily on the MBE, as no English writing is required.

If this strategy works for you, go for it. But remember that while the MBE doesn't require any English writing, it does challenge even native speakers' English reading skills.

Additionally, while essays and MPT's do involve writing in English, keep in mind that the Bar Examiners won't be awarding any points for writing style, grammar, spelling, etc. So long as you can clearly reference the names and elements of the relevant legal concepts, and link them to facts in the essay question, you'll be fine.

Practical Matters

Being trained and/or living overseas creates some very pragmatic issues that need to be sorted out as much in advance of the bar exam as possible.

Bar Requirements

First, you must make sure that you qualify to sit for the bar exam in the jurisdiction you've selected.

Most importantly, you must make sure that the legal education you obtained in your home country qualifies you to take a U.S. state's bar exam.

Depending upon your country and legal education, some states require an LLM degree in order for you to comply with a required number of ABA-accredited law school credits. The situations and circumstances are so varied that I don't want to generalize here for fear of being unintentionally misleading.

The best place to start is the website for the bar you want to join.

Another resource is any major American law school, particularly those with large LLM programs. These schools have administrators who specialize in working with foreign students and most would be happy to talk to you on the telephone or respond to an e-mail.

Immigration Requirements

The second practical matter to sort out is whether you will need any kind of visa to travel to the U.S. jurisdiction you've selected to take the exam.

Again, as each country and person is unique, I can't give any general guidance here. You'll want to check with the relevant governmental bureaus in your home country and then with the U.S. Immigration authorities.

Visiting or contacting a U.S. embassy in your home country can also prove helpful, as, again, can contacting American law schools with a large population of students from overseas.

Spend Some Pre-Exam Time In The Test Location

After all the time, money, and energy you're planning to put into the bar, it would be unfortunate if your exam day performance was harmed by jet lag.

So the third practical matter to sort out is buying your plane ticket and deciding when to arrive and depart.

I'd strongly recommend arriving at least two days before the exam. If you can take the time off and can manage it financially, I think four or five days would be even better, particularly if you're journeying a long distance.

Arriving early allows you to reset your clock so you're in sync with the local time zone.

It also allows you to spend some time trying out different paths to and from your hotel to the test center, timing it so that you know exactly when you should leave your hotel on the test days.

Further, having ample time in the jurisdiction allows you to visit and tour the exam site before the exam days themselves. Not only will familiarity relax you, you can also plot out where the rest rooms are, where you'd like to go for lunch and the quickest way to get there, how cold or hot it's likely to be on the test days so you can dress accordingly, etc.

Chapter 7: For Older Examinees And Those Returning After Time Away From The Law

The bar exam experience is different for older examinees. It's also different for those returning to the law via the bar exam after time away from practice; those who waited several years or more between law school graduation and taking the bar; and those currently practicing who have decided to sit for another jurisdiction's bar exam.

Although some aspects can be more challenging for these test takers, I believe that possessing a few gray hairs and nonlegal professional experiences can be advantageous during the process.

How so? As I stressed in Chapter 5, Maintaining Psychological Sovereignty, the most difficult part of the bar exam is psychologically navigating a stressful and frightening experience.

Older and hopefully wiser, you are perfectly situated to resist the extravaganza of anxiety that bar exam groupthink cultivates, to see through the nervous boasting about scores on sets of practice questions, to ignore the constant mad stream of misinformation about everything from how hard the MBE was during its last administration to how long it takes to be sworn in after receiving a passing score. If you are enrolled in BarBri, you'll be able to talk back to that hysterical compulsive, the Paced Program, and edit it to suit your particular weaknesses, strengths, and schedule.

Balancing Work and Bar Prep

Many older examinees or those currently employed in nonlegal fields don't have the luxury of giving bar prep their undivided attention. Managing the intensity of bar study while continuing to work as usual can be overwhelming, particularly in the final weeks before the exam.

On the other hand, having the structure of a daily work schedule can make getting into a study routine easier. If you work during the day, take a bar prep course that meets at night or online and study both after class and before work in the morning. If you work at night, take the morning class and study during the afternoon. If you get into this groove as soon as bar prep begins, you'll find that this clear structure will keep you steady through to exam days.

Here are some other recommendations for balancing work and bar prep.

Take At Least One Full Week Off Immediately Preceding The Exam

No matter where you are currently working, do your absolute best to clear the last week or two immediately before the exam. As I describe in Chapters 10 and 11, the last two weeks before the exam are crucial to the study process. This is when things really crystallize.

Work Allies

For many reasons, you may be unable to tell those you currently work with that you have embarked upon bar prep and will be taking the bar exam. You may not yet have secured employment in the legal profession and don't want to broadcast that you're about to jump ship. Or you may just not want the added pressure of co-workers continually asking you about the process.

Whatever the circumstances, try to confide in at least a few work buddies. This will give you a bit of emotional support but more importantly a few people who can cover for you when you need to devote more time to bar study.

Plan Ahead

As soon as you decide to take the bar, take a close look at your work schedule for the next three months. Do your best to delay as many projects as possible until after the bar exam. If possible, trade work with co-workers to lighten your load, promising to help them out after the bar exam.

Balancing Family And Bar Prep

As with work, balancing family and bar prep requires planning, open communication, and structure.

Family Meeting

Well before the exam days, sit the whole family together and tell them as much as you can about what lies ahead of you in the next two months of bar prep. With a calendar in front of you, clear as much of the family schedule as possible for the time you'll be studying. Be especially protective of the two weeks immediately preceding the exam.

Acknowledgment

Acknowledge well in advance that your partner and/or children will have to do more around the household during the three months you'll be focused on studying. Think of what you can do after the bar to even the scales.

Involve

You may also enjoy involving your family in your bar prep battle. Depending on the age of any children, you can enlist your son or daughter in the cause and have them quiz you at the dinner table about the finer points of secured transactions or nudge you into following your study schedule if you're tempted to spend a few hours on the couch in front of the television.

No Cramming For You

In Chapter 11, The Last 100 Hours, I discuss "cramming" for the bar—i.e., studying intensely the last few days before the exam after not having kept up with daily work. Although I don't recommend it, I do acknowledge that some do it successfully.

If you have family obligations, I think it's best to avoid cramming. Part of what successfully cramming requires is total freedom from obligations, both personal and professional. It's better suited to the lone wolf than to papa or mama bear.

Welcome Back

If you've been away from the legal profession for a while, or if you chose a nonlegal profession after law school and are now returning to the law and taking the bar, I recommend checking back in with the legal profession.

The most efficient way to do this is to visit internet sites popular in the legal community. "Abovethelaw.com" is a good starting point. You can also surf a number of legal blogs authored by both practicing attorneys and legal academics. A quick Google for "lawyer blog" will get you started.

You should also investigate the Bar Association of the jurisdiction you're sitting for. Most offer frequent seminars and mixers. Even better, you can contact bar members practicing in the areas you want to work in for advice.

Physical Stamina

There is a strong physical component to both bar exam prep and the exam days themselves.

Good physical shape is required to endure long days of study, particularly if you're also attending to work and/or family. This is a great time to begin exercising. Even just 10 or 15 minutes a day will help.

No matter what one's age, the exam days themselves are exhausting. The combination of stress, fatigue, anxiety, and unfamiliar surroundings takes a toll. The better you've been taking care of yourself throughout the process, the easier these days will be to endure. There's more advice about managing the exam days in Chapter 12.

Watch Out For Excuses

Being older and having family or work obligations can also insulate you from some of the helpful, motivating anxiety that flows through the ranks of new JD's. You may start to distance yourself from staying on top of things and using these obligations as excuses for not studying.

To avoid this, try to plan ahead as much as possible, get in the groove of a structured life, and involve your family or confide in a few co-workers as described above so they won't let you make excuses for not studying.

Community

Finally, make friends with other older/non-traditional test takers. You can share strategies about balancing work and study and maintaining family obligations. You can also introduce your families and give your partner, spouse, or kids others to talk to who are also supporting a family member going through the bar exam process.

Chapter 8: Dealing With Family, Friends, And Fellow Examinees

Prepping for the bar is an intense experience. It's good to give some thought to how you'll manage your social life during this time.

All In The Family

Test-takers manage their families in a variety of ways. Some retreat into the family nest for support during the process, while others are providers who run the family nest and have to keep things running smoothly. Here are some of the most common approaches to dealing with family during bar prep.

Checking In To Hotel Mom And Dad

No rent, your own room, and maybe even meals and laundry included? Who would turn that down? Many bar examinees don't. Particularly for those who just graduated from law school, checking in to hotel Mom and Dad just makes sense. Not only will you cut costs and eat well, you'll have the built-in support structure of your family as the pressure mounts.

If You Are Mom Or Dad

If you are Mom or Dad, you will best integrate bar prep into your family obligations if you make a master plan well in advance of the exam days.

If you raised children while in law school, you'll already be familiar with the balancing act here. But the bar exam will ratchet up the pressure and require stamina that even the toughest law school exams didn't.

In the previous chapter, For Older Examinees And Those Returning After Time Away From The Law, I recommend the following strategies for managing family obligations during bar prep:

- Family meeting: Call the family together well in advance of the exam and describe the process as specifically as possible (you can also share this book with them)

- Acknowledgment: Acknowledge in advance that your partner and kids will have to do more than their fair share around the household during your study months; try to plan something fun for the family after the bar
- Involve your kids and/or partner in the study process, helping you make and review flash cards or type up lecture hand-outs

I Love You, Now Leave Me Alone

Whether you are raising children or not, it's best to insulate your relationship with a partner against the up's and down's of bar prep by discussing your expectations and anxieties about the process with them as early as possible.

Try to identify ways you can spend time together while you study and synchronize schedules as much as possible to maximize opportunities for meals, breaks, and emergency vacations.

If you are experiencing relationship problems with your partner, the intensity of bar exam prep can intensify them. They can also get in the way of successful bar prep. If possible, and if palatable to your temperament, try to structure a break or detente to coincide with the bar prep process.

If you stay in the problematic relationship until pretty far into bar prep without such a break, it's probably best not to make any large relationship decisions until after the exam.

With Friends Like These . . .

Hopefully you have some good friends taking the bar with you. These should be one of your principal support groups, and they are discussed later under the heading Law School Chums. These are not the friends referenced immediately below. Here are some common types of non-bar taking friends, and how they may react to your entering the tunnel of bar exam study.

The Tempter/Temptress

The Tempter/Temptress is the friend who refuses to take your bar exam prep seriously and encourages you to skip lectures and betray study schedules in order to participate in fun activities such as dining, shooting hoops, going to movies, etc.

This is usually done for one of three reasons. First, the Tempter may truly be ignorant about the enormous scope of material covered by the bar exam and the necessity of structured study. Second, the Temptress may have always viewed you as a super-smart academic star who went to law school and would of course ace the bar exam without problem. Nothing you say will convince her otherwise. Finally, and probably unbeknownst to himself, the Tempter may be a little jealous at your imminent societal upgrade to attorney.

The best way to deal with the Tempter/Temptress type of friend is to enlist them in helping you make plans to celebrate your completion of the bar exam. The Tempter is at heart a fun-loving type who will look forward to such revels.

The Party Animal

The Party Animal is usually a part of the mix for younger examinees, and sometimes for older ones. We are all familiar with the Party Animal's primary objective in life: drinking, carousing, and general mayhem.

While there are many die-hard party animals, sometimes friends may change into Party Animals seemingly overnight as a way of managing a new life stress or escaping a difficult interpersonal situation.

Do your best to steer clear of either kind of Party Animal during the duration of your study. Particularly during the last month, a few hangovers can really start to derail things.

Of course, once the exam is over, it may be time to get reacquainted with this type of friend.

The Solid Supporter

Ah, the Solid Supporter. Hopefully you have one or two. The Solid Supporter is often a spouse, partner, sibling, therapist, or friend.

The Solid Supporter just gets it. He or she understands the intense nature of the bar prep experience. He or she won't try to tempt you into partying or cheating on your study schedule.

Should you find yourself experiencing an up-swing in anxiety, the Solid Supporter is always a first call.

Meeting up with a Supporter for a brief, fun activity also makes an excellent Emergency Vacation.

The Veteran

One of the best kinds of Solid Supporters, The Veteran deserves a heading of her own.

The veteran is a friend of yours who is a practicing attorney who successfully passed the bar within the last five years or so.

Like a seasoned officer giving advice to a new recruit, the veteran will understand where you are in the bar study process. He will confide in you that he experienced the same fears and the same feelings of hopelessness that you may be experiencing. She will soothe you with stories about her own mismanagement of her study time in the final weeks and the topics she didn't prepare at all. When you get closer to the exam days, the veteran will tell you about her own sense of having messed up numerous essay questions, about the sense that the MBE questions were far more difficult than any of the practice or released ones, or the session where he'd discovered he'd miscoded an entire row of answer ovals with only five minutes left.

And one day soon, hopefully, you can play the Veteran to a struggling bar prepping friend of yours. Bar prep karma.

Brothers And Sisters In Arms

Your fellow bar examinees will be both a blessing and a curse to you. Blessing in that they'll offer a community of people undergoing the same stresses as they attempt to digest so much legal material in such a brief period of time. Curse in that they are in a sense competitors in what can feel like a tournament.

Here's a head's-up on some of the types of examinees you can expect so you'll be prepared to manage them.

Law School Chums

If you've just graduated and are fortunate enough to be in a bar prep course with friends from your law school class, consider yourself lucky. You have a built-in support structure and camaraderie. Assuming you decide to take a prep course that meets at a brick and mortar location, you will feel reassured every time you walk into the classroom and see some familiar faces.

Once the prep course ends, these former classmates will be good people to call when you need to check in with someone undergoing the same experience.

The Whiz Kid

It's unlikely that you've gotten this far in your academic career without meeting this common type. The Whiz Kid will dazzle you with the multicolored Post-It flags heralding the sections of his outline. He or she will ask probing questions about the material covered in a way which showcases obvious time spent studying and memorizing the night before. He or she will also discuss all elements of the bar exam, from her opinions about the statistical variations in recent bar passage rates to a studied mistrust of Subject Frequency Charts which suggests an ambition to be unremittingly comprehensive.

While the Whiz Kid's intensity may grate on you, he or she is also a valuable source of information about any confusion you may have over the legal material covered during a lecture or practice MBE questions you find confounding.

And, come on, you've made it through law school, you will make it through the bar—you're a bit of a whiz kid too, aren't you?

The Kings Or Queens Of Anxiety

You probably have encountered this type before. In fact, because you've been drawn to the legal profession, you most likely have some neurotic tendencies yourself. In a good, don't-miss-that-filing-deadline kind of way, of course.

The Kings or Queens of Anxiety take things much further. These bedeviled examinees cultivate anxiety and spend a great deal of time contemplating worst case scenarios and relishing a self-created ambience of imminent doom.

The danger of these Kings and Queens is that their anxiety can become contagious. At a time when all examinees are struggling to manage a certain amount of anxiety, these anxiety-loving test-takers can often successfully seed doubts into your mind.

To resist this, remain centered. Stick to your study plan and remind yourself that these kings and queens are not the voice of reason, but merely anxious test-takers interacting with their anxieties as a coping mechanism.

The Slacker

The Slacker is the opposite of the anxious royals and sometimes a tempter or whiz kid in disguise.

He or she will openly mock the bar prep course proceedings, routinely arrive late and leave early, and boast about not having yet done any reading or note synthesizing. He or she will refuse any serious conversation about the exam and will be disdainful of the fears of others.

Slackers are often fun, interesting people, but they can endanger your commitment to your study plan. Like the tempter, some slackers will make persuasive arguments in favor of blowing off work, such as "I'm not going to remember anything I hear now in lecture in a month and a half, so why bother paying attention?" Actually, there's very good reason to bother, as this first pass at the material will lay the ground track for future study. (This is discussed further in the next chapter, Daily Work.)

Slackers can also be Whiz Kids in disguise. For some of them, bar prep is a relative breeze.

Maybe they possess unusually strong memories or are just particularly adept at distilling large amounts of new information. Whatever their hidden talents may be, Slackers are not good guides for the majority of examinees as their false sense of security can be seductive and ultimately detrimental to staying on track.

Examinees In Love

Yes, it happens. Two bar examinees, prepping to sit for the same bar exam, who are romantically involved. Maybe even living together.

Is this a very good idea? Or perhaps a very bad one?

That depends on the amount of communication between the couple both before and during bar prep.

I'd suggest starting with an honest assessment of the potential for collaboration. Not all romantic partners make good study partners. Even if the test-takers have gone to law school together, the bar exam is different in the uniformity of the subject matter covered and the enormity of the experience. Ask yourselves if your study styles mesh, and try to be as frank as possible. If they do, great. You can split up some of the bar prep tasks. But if they don't—if one of you is a daily worker and the other more of a crammer, for example—try to find ways to permit each partner to have an independent bar study journey while still taking advantage of the built-in support of someone who really knows what you are going through.

You may also want to diagnose the overall health of the relationship. If things are not going well before bar prep, the intensity of both of you simultaneously prepping for the same bar may stress things to the breaking point.

On the other hand, maybe it will provide the emergency resuscitation a flagging relationship requires.

Whatever the case, planning ahead, talking things through, and taking honest stock of all aspects of the situation will help.

Man's Best Friend

In addition to the company of friends, family, and partners, pets can make wonderful bar exam preparation companions.

Not only is it well-known that pets have a calming effect on the anxieties of their human handlers, but the routine walking and overall structure of pet ownership duties can help in creating a study routine.

When I studied, I frequently rewarded myself with dog walks. During a freezing cold Boston winter these walks were bracing and rejuvenating experiences.

At home, my dog played Bar Examiner with quiet, engaged attention as I attempted to vocalize some of the finer points of future interests. Even better, he didn't seem to know whether or not I knew what I was talking about. Which usually made two of us.

Chapter 9: Daily Work

The following three chapters include recommendations on how to manage the daily work of bar exam preparation.

This chapter focuses on the bulk of your preparation, and presumes that like nearly all examinees, you are enrolled in some kind of prep course. If you're the rare independent thinker who prefers to fly solo, merely substitute references to course work with your own home schooling schedule.

Chapter 10 covers the last two weeks or so of preparation between the end of most bar courses and the examination days.

Finally, Chapter 11 addresses the final 100 hours of self-study immediately preceding the exam.

Congratulations, You've Just Been Promoted To Paralegal

When I worked as a summer associate at a Wall Street law firm I was amazed by how much of a corporate lawyer's work was clerical. The highlight of my rotation through one of the finance groups was being granted the responsibility of assembling a Closing List—a catalog of all the documents that needed to be assembled for the close of a big deal. From pledge agreements to legal opinions, there were hundreds of papers to track down from dozens of sources and arrange on a massive table in a conference room.

Although I worked in numerous departments on qualitatively different transactions, I came to appreciate the central importance of good document management skills.

The same goes for bar exam preparation.

I encourage you to take some time at the beginning of your studying process to get yourself organized.

Here are some concrete recommendations:

- Buy 6 binders with interior pockets, one for each of the six Multistate Subjects, and preferably each a different color.
- Label the binders on both the front and sides with the subject name.
- Put everything relating to each Multistate subject into its binder: the lecture handouts, the local distinctions, the Fine Points summaries, and, eventually, your condensed notes.
- In the pocket of each Multistate binder, put the Conviser Mini Review pages for that subject (preferably stapled together and

bound with masking tape into little portable pamphlets).

- Use different colored binders, and feel free to get creative and add stickers, artwork, etc. to the covers so that each binder-subject develops a unique personality.
- Buy an additional 2 binders, jumbo-sized, and several packs of tabbed dividers.
- Label the dividers with each of the local subjects, insert them into the big binders, and use them to arrange all materials relating to the local subjects, including lecture handouts, Fine Points, condensed notes, charts, etc.

Depending on the jurisdiction in which you're sitting for the exam and how you choose to categorize the law, you'll have as many as twenty legal topics with which to familiarize yourself before exam day. This can be initially quite frightening. I remember muttering to myself the eighteen topics on the Massachusetts bar like some sort of crazy catechism, as if merely knowing what topics would be covered would provide me with secret powers.

Organizing the materials into binders at the outset will start to give you a sense of control over the awesome amount of law covered on the bar exam. The binders are the first step in providing a structure for each topic. External at first, this structure will ultimately be mirrored in your mind, as you maintain interior, mental binders within the confines of your skull that you will bring with you to the examination days.

Bueller . . . Bueller . . . Bueller . . .

Don't be Ferris from *Ferris Bueller's Day Off*.

In other words, attend class. Every day. Whether live or video or online streaming.

Bring the Mad Libs-like fill-in-the-blank handouts with you and dutifully fill them out like a moron.

Don't worry if you fall behind in the sets of practice questions assigned by that demented compulsive, The Paced Program. Don't worry if you miss online Multistate workshops, or fall behind in the reading, or haven't even started condensing your notes although weeks have gone by since the course started.

But if you start missing class, be concerned. Not so concerned that you freak out and aren't capable of making a plan to catch up. But concerned enough that you don't miss class repeatedly.

Beware of letting the mere presence of the lectures online lull you into a false sense of security. It's difficult to catch up when you have missed three or more lectures. As each lecture averages a little over three hours, it would take more than a full day of solid lecture watching to make up three missed ones.

As I wrote above, the few times I tried to polish off more than two online streaming lectures in a day, I found it painful and exhausting. Despite the fact that I was comfortably ensconced in my favorite desk chair before my iMac at home, with coffee, snacks, and a sleeping dog, my mind simply couldn't take it, especially after the sixth hour.

Another problem with falling behind in lectures while your mind weaves the wild alibi of one day catching up on all of them is that it retards your ability to begin the crucial process of condensing your notes as you prepare your final review document.

If you have a poor track record of attending class in law school—even if you did well in the classes you most often skipped—I'd strongly suggest signing up for a live or DVD location where you can get into the habit of being physically present every day.

If you do pull a few Buellers, don't have a meltdown. Just make up the lectures online as soon as possible, prioritizing catching up above all other studying activities.

Practice MBE Questions

The 200 question, six hour Multistate Bar Exam is an extremely difficult test. In fact, I can't think of a more difficult multiple choice exam administered routinely in the United States.

Our future defendants in the medical profession have it easier. Medical examinations tend to be specialized and therefore cover far less material. By contrast the Multistate covers all aspects of the law. Know for a fact that you will never engage as an attorney with the criminal justice system? Too bad, you'll be tested on Criminal Law and Procedure anyway. No interest in being a Constitutional Law scholar? Sorry, you'll be examined on Con Law anyway. No plans to be a trial attorney? Apologies, but you'll still be quizzed on the law of Evidence.

However, the fact that the MBE is so challenging shouldn't make you tremble in your Tevas, but rather relax you. Why? For the simple reason that you and your fellow examinees can get so many questions incorrect and still pass the bar exam.

As I've already emphasized, we're talking roughly 70 wrong for the average passing candidate, assuming an equally average score on the local day. And this doesn't include the 10 experimental questions on the MBE that don't count at all.

So it is very important at the outset to view the MBE not as an exam you must dominate or master, but rather as an exam that you only have to do a little better than 50% on.

This view flies in the face of the scholastically sophisticated personalities most law schools attract. Can you imagine heading into a law school exam aiming for the equivalent of an F? Or celebrating if you received a D, or, miracle of miracles, a C? (Those of you unfortunate souls who, like me, took Secured Transactions may indeed have little trouble imagining this.)

Grounded in this point of view, approach the MBE practice sets you do accordingly.

At first, as I did, you may do really, really badly on them. I'm talking like two or three right out of twenty.

Do not be alarmed by this. You have to start somewhere. If you were acing these practice questions, you'd have nowhere to go but down, and that wouldn't be so much fun.

More importantly, think of yourself as starting a relationship with an extremely dysfunctional, evasive, and confusing mate. Your first few dates with the MBE are likely to go terribly. You're a nice, open person I'm sure, but the MBE is not. The MBE is the kind of partner who will try to trick you with wrong answers that sound legally authoritative—some of them even sporting Latin phrases.

Although you'll be assisted by your ever-increasing knowledge of the law, you'll be helped equally by your ever-increasing knowledge of the demented personality of the MBE.

Thankfully, like most dysfunctional people, the MBE resorts to the same kind of behavior again and again. Once you start to decipher these patterns, the exam can be downright predictable at times.

As the saying goes: Fool me once, shame on you; fool me twice, shame on me.

Aside from getting familiar with the personality style of the MBE, another benefit to doing practice questions is reading the answer explanations afterwards.

It's tempting to skip this part altogether, or only read the answer explanations for the questions you get wrong.

But I'd recommend reading all of the answers to all of the questions, as time permits. This achieves two purposes simultaneously: It allows you to understand the tricks behind many of the answer choices on the MBE, and it allows you to start reviewing not only the law tested by the question, but other law that frequently confuses you about the law tested.

I also recommend buying a stand-alone timer so you get used to the slightly less than two minute per question pace you'll need for the exam. These are widely available and cheap. I bought one on Amazon for less than ten dollars.

Practice Essays

While practice MBE questions can be kind of fun (within the mind-numbing context of bar exam preparation, of course), practice essay questions are time-consuming and intimidating.

Particularly at first, when you haven't yet studied the relevant law, much less begun to memorize anything, reading through practice essays can be terrifying. Is it really possible that within eight weeks or less you'll be able to write coherent and informative responses that will allow you to pass the bar?

The answer to this question is a resounding YES. Just as with the first rounds of MBE questions you endeavor, the first dozen essays you try may leave you in a state of doubt and hopelessness.

This is perfectly normal. If you were kicking butt on these questions, why would you be spending the next eight to ten weeks studying?

I found that for me and many of my fellow examinees, essay performance crystallized the latest of all bar exam skills. As covered above, the MBE is a dysfunctional personality whose patterns become predictable over time. Even if you don't know the law, after a few weeks you will start to be able to delete potential answer choices.

Essays are more challenging because there's no wrong law to eliminate. Everything has to flow from your pen.

What I found most helpful about doing practice essays was reading the model answers. Not only did they help me learn what law applied in what context, they modeled the bar exam essay "voice" I started to emulate.

Once you start to get the voice down, you can then plug in the appropriate law and details from the fact patterns.

So my recommendation is that you read through practice essay questions and their answers quickly at first. Don't get bogged down, and don't get nervous. If you're pressed for time, always skip the practice essays in favor of making sure to attend all lectures and starting to condense your notes.

One caveat. If you are a foreign-born examinee who has difficulty writing in English, or if you are an American JD with an aversion to writing, devote much more time to essay practice. For you, the actual writing of the essays may require more practice than for others, and you may want to write out full answers instead of merely outlining or scanning through the questions and model responses.

Multistate Performance Test: Let's Play Make-Believe Lawyer

Some but not all jurisdictions now include a relatively new species of bar exam testing, the bizarrely named Multistate Performance Test, or MPT. This testing module is part of the local essay day in the jurisdictions in which it appears. It is designed, written, and graded by the same wonderful folks who prepare and grade the MBE, and purchased by the states that utilize it.

After taking the Massachusetts Bar, which does not use the MPT, I initially viewed the MPT on the New York Bar with fear and mistrust (a reasonable initial response to any component of the bar exam, don't you think?). But the more I learned about it, the more I came to like it. By the end of my bar preparation, I was actually grateful for its presence on the NY Bar.

"Grateful!" I hear you exclaiming in astonishment and horror. How could I be grateful about any component of the bar exam?

Here's why. The MPT requires no legal knowledge whatsoever. Want me to repeat that? Here is a full list of all of the legal topics covered by the MPT: none. One more time: zero.

Instead, the MPT tests soft skills such as your ability to research case law and write a memo. In other words, if your jurisdiction offers the MPT, you'll get to spend an hour and a half of your bar examination playing make-believe lawyer.

Isn't that preferable to another two essay questions testing your recall of, say, the law of corporations or the minutiae of commercial paper? I certainly think so.

So am I recommending that you do no preparation for the MPT?

Almost. I would recommend that you read through some past MPT questions and sample answers. The easiest way to score astronomically high on the MPT is to fastidiously use headings and numbered sections as you write your pretend memo, brief, or closing argument. Be obsessively organized in your writing, as if your reader has a terrible memory and keeps on forgetting where you are in your presentation and what you just previously addressed and are on the brink of addressing.

Also, as I mentioned in the essay writing section above, if you're generally not comfortable writing essays or are not a native English-speaker, you may want to spend a good deal more time writing out practice MPT's.

Local Day Multiple Choice Or Short-Answer? Lucky You.

When I prepared for the Massachusetts bar, I remember being happy that the Commonwealth did not feel a need to torture its aspiring lawyers with local day, state-specific multiple choice or short answer questions. Sometimes I would think of the unlucky examinees in other jurisdictions who not only had to experience the stresses I did, but also somehow deal with these state day zingers.

Well, when preparing for the New York bar exam, I was now one of those unlucky examinees I had previously pitied. The NY bar has 50 local day multiple choice questions with a recommended testing time of 1hr.

What on earth was I going to do?

My strategy here was to do relatively little. Why?

Although both the MBE and the local day questions were multiple choice, there was a major difference between them. Whereas the MBE questions are tricky and full of distracting and confusing answers that you might be tempted to choose even when you know the relevant law like the back of your hand, the local day multiple choice questions don't try to trick you. They are straightforward tests of your legal knowledge.

Once I realized this, I realized something else: There was no point in even practicing the local day questions until near the end of my bar exam preparation, because until then I wouldn't know much of the required law.

I recommend you do the same with local day multiple choice and short answer. Don't freak yourself out by trying them too early when you don't know the local law.

On the actual day of the NY Bar exam, I found the local day questions refreshingly direct in comparison to the difficult MBE. Of course I didn't know the answers to all the questions, but at least I didn't have to play mental chess with the way the questions themselves were asked.

There is one comforting similarity between the MBE and the local multiple choice questions in many jurisdictions. In New York, the average passing candidate gets only 25 out of 50 questions correct. Think you got ten wrong in a row? Doesn't matter, you could still kick butt. Put answer "B" for the first 20 questions without reading them? No problem, you can still be successful on this portion of the test.

Since the local day multiple choice are not tricky, and because most people who pass get half of them wrong, feel confident as you choose to delay the start of your preparation for these questions. Most likely, with some local law under your belt, you too will find this section of the bar exam surprisingly refreshing and straight-forward.

Condense Your Lecture Handouts Into A Final Review Document

In terms of pure nuts-and-bolts strategy, the heading above is the most important advice I have for you.

The second most important piece of advice is related, and covered in the next chapter: Stop condensing your notes about two weeks (or at the very latest, one week) before the exam itself.

Condensing your lecture handouts and notes is crucial because some subjects, such as Property, have handouts that approach a hundred pages or more. As you add up the six Multistate subjects (and Criminal Law is really two subjects in one, both law and procedure), and then add the local day, you'll see with some surprise that you're dealing with over a thousand pages of handouts.

The problem is that it's impossible to study and somewhat memorize that much material.

A big part of the bar exam preparation process is whittling down your material bit by bit until you are left with the Holy Grail—your Final Review Document. This is the most grueling, mind-numbing, and exhausting part of bar exam prep. But once you're done, you can spend your remaining time reading through your Holy Grail until you can quote scripture and verse.

How To Condense Your Notes

So how exactly do you go about this condensing business?

I recommend you follow these steps:

Estimate The Ideal Document Length For Each Subject

Before you begin condensing, imagine in your mind the ideal Final Review Document for each subject. Some topics, such as Property, will require more pages than others, such as Contracts.

It's difficult to give exact page length recommendations because so many factors influence how many words are on a page: handwriting vs. typing, font size and spacing, etc.

Personally, I aimed for between ten and twenty typed pages for each Multistate subject, and less than five for most local subjects (with a few exceptions such as New York Practice and Wills.)

Continually keep in mind how many pages you'll feel comfortable trying to master in the final days before the exam. Your aim should be to have all the information you need about every topic somewhere within your final outline.

No More Time For Hypotheticals

As you read through your fill-in-the-blank lecture handouts, you'll notice that at least 25% of them—and, for many subjects, more than 50%—are made up of hypotheticals. These multi-paragraph fill-in-the-blank fact patterns are used by lecturers to bring the black letter to interactive life so examinees can understand how to operationalize them on the exam.

But once you've read through them a few times, hypotheticals should be the first part of the lecture handouts you eliminate as you condense your notes.

If there are brief hypos you find useful in helping you remember the law, by all means include them in your final review document.

As for the rest, skip over them gleefully as you create your svelte Final Review Document masterpiece.

Thinking In Pictures

Certain bar exam subjects such as Property, Evidence, and Constitutional Law are particularly well-suited to charts. If you are a visual thinker, I recommend Xeroxing (or scanning in) the most helpful charts from the lecture handouts and appending them to your final review documents.

The goal is to go "off-handout" completely. If you hope to flip back and forth between your final outline and the handouts in order to consult charts, you're defeating the whole purpose.

Also, if you're not a visual thinker and don't respond to charts, say, comparing the future interests, defeasible fees, or hearsay exceptions, then by all means skip over them. Reduce, reduce, reduce, wherever and whenever you can.

Do It Alone

If in law school you used outlines to prepare for final exams, you already have a certain amount of experience in creating a Final Review Document.

As you most likely found then, a good part of the learning occurred during the process of assembling the outline, even if it wasn't entirely obvious at the time. As you created your outline sections and sub-sections, you were subconsciously laying down a base track of knowledge in your mind that would be reinforced with subsequent review.

If you ever tried to study from someone else's finished outline, you may have wondered why it wasn't as effective. Perhaps you were in a study group 1L year in which you split up the work of making final outlines. Did you notice that you always seemed more comfortable with the outlines you yourself created? When using someone else's review document, did you sometimes scratch your head in confusion, not understanding their structure or the way they had condensed certain topics?

For all these reasons, I strongly suggest you make your own Final Review Document in preparation for the bar exam.

Some of the BarBri professors encourage students to use their lecture handouts for final review. This is a fine last resort (covered in the next chapter), but not something to shoot for. Why? Because these professors seem to have forgotten that their 60–page outline doesn't exist in a vacuum, and that other professors' handouts run 80, 90, 100 pages or more.

You've Been Drafted

Condensing isn't easy. Deciding what to leave in and what to leave out can be excruciating. On the one hand, you certainly don't want to leave out any law that has a high likelihood of being tested on your bar exam. On the other hand, you don't want to end up with a Final

Review Document that is nearly as long as the handouts it's intended to replace.

The main way I dealt with this was to conceptualize creating my Final Review Document as a multi-draft procedure.

The purpose of the first draft was to free myself from the enormous handouts.

Then, in successive drafts, I would start pruning away all excesses until I was eventually left with the amount of pages I'd aimed for.

Writing in drafts with continual pruning also provides the benefit of helping you learn the law. Each time you work through your outline and cut as much as possible, you become more familiar with the contours of what remains.

By the time you reach the final draft, you'll be amazed by how familiar you've become with it.

Mr. Television Man

As I've emphasized, condensing your notes is not only crucial, but a beast of a task. It's much easier to pop off a few MBE practice questions or read through model essay answers.

When I started to condense my New York Practice notes, I bribed myself into working by allowing myself to keep the television on in the background. This helped a lot.

Make this same deal with yourself. Permit yourself to play your favorite music, or DVD's of *Curb Your Enthusiasm* or *Entourage*—whatever media you enjoy the most—so long as you keep on chugging along with your outline.

Priorities

In sum, here are the steps I've recommended taking as you do your daily work:

- Get yourself organized
- Attend all lectures
- Condense your notes
- Do practice MBE questions and review the answers
- Read through model essay answers
- Once you've encountered the local law, try some local multiple choice/short answer but don't fixate

- Briefly scan released MPT questions and answers if you're lucky enough to have this component on your bar

Chapter 10: The Final Two Weeks

Two Week Warning

Ah, the final two weeks. Take heart, brave examinee, just 14 more days until your bar exam adventure comes to a close.

At this point, your prep course has ended or will shortly.

Suddenly it'll dawn on you that the only thing worse than having to go to lecture every day is realizing that there is no more class, that the bar exam is fast approaching, and that the rest of the studying process is up to you and you alone.

A sudden upswing in anxiety for even the biggest Paced Program nerd is perfectly understandable at this point. Here are a few things to remember to help you maintain psychological sovereignty.

You've Learned More Than You Realize

It's highly likely that the hundreds of hours you spent sitting through BarBri lectures filling in the blanks of lecture handouts were not the most thrilling times of your life.

But what you may not have realized at this point is that, to a certain degree, you have been successfully brainwashed. Even if you were on auto-pilot much of the time, just passively receiving the black letter flying out at you, your brain has taken in some of the material, and you have reinforced this subconscious absorption while reviewing and condensing your notes.

It's similar to the way you might find yourself suddenly able to sing along with a pop song you've heard a few times while driving or at a club. While never consciously sitting down with the lyrics and setting about the task of memorizing them, you've learned them.

You may find this happening on the bar exam—not singing pop lyrics, which fellow examinees in the convention hall may not find amusing, but suddenly finding yourself writing out, say, the four components of Adverse

Possession, even though you technically never set about actively memorizing them.

It All Will Start Coming Together: Believe!

Both times I prepared for the bar exam, everything started coming together during the last two weeks. This isn't to say that I felt confident. Quite the contrary, I, like I'm sure many of you at this point, felt that I was doomed to fail and spend eternity in a BarBri purgatory, listening to the same lectures again and again.

It just kind of happened, in ways I didn't realize until the actual bar exam itself, when I found myself writing essays about formerly terrifying topics such as wills and future interests or able to cross out at least some of the wrong answer choices on the MBE with a refreshing confidence.

I'm not encouraging you to continually monitor yourself to see if the Great Legal Enlightenment has occurred for you yet.

At this point, I'd just like you to cultivate something like faith, or trust—or at the very least dim hope—that you will experience it too like all the other bar examinees who have traveled the lonely bar prep road before you.

The End Is Near

There's one other silver lining to the rush of anxiety you may experience as the two exam days approach: You can see the light at the end of the tunnel.

"Two weeks and two days from today," I used to think, "It'll all be over."

If you've planned a well-earned post-bar trip, fire up your screensavers with pictures of your destination: Amsterdam? Paris? Sedona? Tahiti? Mexico? Hoboken?

If you haven't planned a trip, imagining the sudden weight of bar prep lifting from your shoulders is most likely heavenly enough by this point.

Over are the early weeks of bar prep, when you may have felt like you were stepping into the quicksand of black letter law and endless lectures.

Over too is the middle period, coinciding with the hottest days of summer (or the coldest days of winter), a timeless spaceless interzone where many examinees start to forget why they chose the legal profession and wonder if it's time to dust off that half-written novel from freshman year of college.

Now you're officially in the End Zone. Welcome. Don't forget to temper any increasing anxiety with an appreciation for how far you've come. Even if you blew off practice question sets and practice essays, your mere endurance to this point is a real achievement.

Condensation Overload

In the previous chapter I emphasized the importance of condensing your notes into a Final Review Document.

But, At This Point, Stop Condensing, Even If You're Not Done

I learned this the hard way. When I prepared for the Massachusetts Bar, I kept on condensing my notes until just a few short days before the exam itself. Ironically, I spent so much time condensing my notes that I never got a chance to read through some of the condensed versions. I remember sitting on a bench near the modernistic Boston City Hall an hour before the local essay day began, scanning for the first time the condensed outlines I'd made for Family Law, Wills, Trusts, and Corporations.

When I took the NY Bar, I promised myself I wouldn't make the same mistake. Although I wasn't done condensing some of the local topics, including some major ones like Wills, I stopped condensing my notes and started reading through the ones I had condensed multiple times. For the topics I hadn't condensed, I just used the handouts I'd filled out during the BarBri lecture. Some of the BarBri lecturers encourage you to use their fill-in-the-blank outlines as final review documents. While I still think it's best to make your own condensed versions, doing your final review from the handouts for the subjects you didn't have time to condense beats spending too much time condensing new topics in the days before the exam.

Visual Editing

When forced to do final review from BarBri (or other prep course) fill-in-the-blank handouts, I recommend reading through it quickly once, hypotheticals and all, and then, on further readings, skipping the hypotheticals in favor of the black letter. What you'll realize is that the bulk of the BarBri in-class outlines are hypos. As I mentioned above, a large part of condensing is leaving out the lengthy hypos, except when they compactly illustrate a point of law you still find puzzling. As you speed through the outlines multiple times, you'll find that even the longest ones become much more manageable when you visually edit out the excess material.

Read, Re-Read, Re-Re-Read . . .

So if you shouldn't be spending any more time condensing your notes, what should you be doing?

In a word: reading. Read your Final Review Document (or read any remaining uncondensed handouts by visually editing as explained above).

Some people are nutty for flashcards. This method doesn't help me personally and I worry that the process of making flashcards can take up time better spent studying a Final Review

Document. But if flashcards are your thing, by all means, go nuts with flashcards.

For me, during the last two weeks of bar prep before both the New York and Massachusetts bar exams, what really helped me to bring it all together was to read my condensed notes again and again and again.

At this point in the process, you'll find the distinction between reading and memorization gets blurred. The more you read, say, your contracts notes, the more you'll find yourself able to recall what types of contracts fall within the Statute of Frauds.

So should you ever sit down and expressly try to memorize anything?

I think this depends on your learning style. I'd try experimenting a bit with both repeated read-throughs and memorization to find the mixture that works best for you.

Do Not Betray Your Holy Grail

Remember, at this point in the process, your Final Review Document is your Holy Grail.

What does this mean?

Now is not the time to consult the Big Bastards for anything. Nor should you visit Conviserland for anything but the briefest of stays to clarify a point or two.

At the two week mark, I'd recommend becoming comfortable with a new skill: letting things go. Still don't get the Rule Against Perpetuities? Then just drop it. You're better off at this point continuing your read-throughs of your condensed notes than struggling through the complexities of law you find difficult.

You may want to continue doing practice MBE—and, as the test day gets closer, practice local questions to keep yourself in the game.

But now is not the time to try to make up all the practice questions you may have missed during your prep course, or to seek out more and more questions to do.

Overall, repeated reading and review of your condensed notes will help you with all sections of the bar exam, both essay and standardized, as your legal knowledge increases.

This is the integrated knowledge you've been working towards since you started bar prep.

Game Plan

At some point during these last two weeks, make a clear time management game plan for the two days of testing, and commit to it.

Aside from actual legal knowledge and familiarity with the dysfunctional personality of the MBE, time management is the most critical skill on the bar exam. Make a plan and do your best to stick to it no matter how distracted you get by a particularly difficult essay fact pattern or series of Multistate questions.

Part of your game plan should include explicit strategies for not getting bogged down and how to spend any remaining time.

For example, my not-getting-bogged-down strategy for the MBE was to stick to a little less than 2 minutes per question, to record an answer for every question the first time around, and to circle questions in the examination book I felt particularly unsure about to return to if I had any remaining time.

For the local day, a time management game plan depends upon the structure of the exam in your jurisdiction. The Massachusetts local day consisted of 10 essays, five in the morning and five in the afternoon. Both sessions were 3 hours long. Equally divided, this gave me 36 minutes per essay. To give myself a few extra minutes, I rounded this down to 35 minutes per essay. I then divided this 35 minute parcel of time per essay into 15 minutes for reading and outlining and 20 minutes for writing. During the exam, I stuck to this time schedule, and I was always sure to leave a full page of blank space at the end of each essay answer to return to if I had remaining minutes and wanted to make additions before time was called.

The New York Bar local day was a little trickier, as it features essays, local day multiple choice, and the Multistate Performance Test. Specifically, the morning session lasts for 3hrs and 15 minutes and contains three essays and 50 local multiple choice questions. The afternoon session lasts 3hrs and contains two essays and the MPT.

Since I wanted to get the multiple choice questions out of the way, I did that section first, even though it appeared last in the question booklet. I gave myself 1 hour and 15 minutes for the multiple choice, around one and a half minutes per question. This left me with two hours for the three essays, or 40 minutes each. I divided the 40 minute parcel of time per essay into 15 minutes for reading and outlining, and 25 minutes for writing. Once again, I left a full blank page at the end of each essay answer to return to if I had remaining minutes and wanted to make additions.

In the afternoon, I used the same 40 minute approach to the two remaining essays. I then gave an hour and a half to the MPT. This left me with an "extra" 10 minutes to play around with. Since this was, for New York, the last session of the first day of the exam, I knew it was likely that fatigue was going to start setting in and it would be nice to cushion my game plan with an extra 10 minutes.

Once you've devised your game plan, make sure you've memorized it so that you don't have to waste any time during the actual exam figuring out what you're going to do and in what order.

Avoid The Up-Sell

In the final weeks before the bar exam, you'll find that your bar prep course will besiege you with offers to purchase additional review products for the final days before the exam.

These often take the form of all-day review lectures at live locations within a week of examination day.

Resist these capitalistic siren calls aimed at your anxiety and pocketbook.

At this point in the process, no activity will reap more dividends than doing your best to master your Final Review Document. The last thing you need now is to deal with a bunch of neurotic fellow examinees and a new lecturer with a new spin on black letter.

It's tempting and perfectly understandable that, while reaching for your Discover card to sign up, you could rationalize that purchasing and attending these last minute review courses will be helpful. The marketing materials for these products may try to convince you that it would be downright treacherous to do otherwise.

Resist. With your game plan and Holy Grail, you will be prepared.

Avoid Other Peoples' Study Aids And Advice

The final weeks before the examination, you'll most likely encounter fellow examinees who will trumpet their possession of a cornucopia of secret study aids or "cheats" to the most feared bar exam topics.

The more magnanimous among them may offer to e-mail them to you in attachments so that you may be similarly enlightened.

You'll also encounter fellow examinees who have become dime store prophets. "It's definitely gonna be conflict of laws on essay day," they'll predict to anyone who'll listen. "It's been seven point five years since conflicts have appeared on the exam so it's definitely due."

Or, "I have a friend who told me that the MBE's gonna be a lot harder this year because the pass rate was too high last year."

Or, "I heard that the Bar Examiners are going to reduce the amount of time we have for each session of the local essay day from three hours to one hour to see how we deal with the unexpected."

Ignore these prophets, politely refuse the secret study aids, and stick to your Final Review Document.

At this point in the bar exam preparation process, less truly is more.

Take Care Of Yourself

Imagine this. The last two weeks before the two test days, you pushed yourself to the limit studying.

"This is it," you reasoned. "I'm going to study 20 hours a day every day for the next two weeks. I can sleep the whole month of August (or March)."

Conjuring all the discipline and endurance within you, you follow through on your plan and study black letter like it's going out of style.

You never get more than four hours of sleep, your coffee maker is working so much overtime it's contemplating unionization, and your neighbors start to wonder if aliens have hatched zombie eggs in your brain.

The night before the first day of the bar, you feel a tickle in your throat and notice that your forehead is hot enough to fry bacon on.

You wake the day of the exam to find yourself feverish, your throat ablaze with soreness. Aches and pains travel through your legs, your back, your arms.

You travel to the test site in a fog. As you wait for the lead proctor to announce that you may break the seal on the examination book, you notice that your shirt is soaked through with sweat. You are certain that the proctor assigned to your section either is E.T., the famous extraterrestrial, or bears such a striking resemblance that he could clean up in Vegas as a celebrity impersonator.

The exam begins, and a few minutes into the MBE you hear someone shouting near you "My name is Marvin and I'm from Mars!" Then you realize that that person is *you*. E.T. rushes over, surely excited by the prospect of meeting another intergalactic being.

Everything goes black. When you awaken in a hospital room, the nurse explains that you fainted at the exam center. The bad news is you'll have to prep all over again and take the bar exam at the next administration. The good news is that in an informal straw poll during break, your fellow examinees at the test center granted you the prestigious (and highly competitive) award for Most Entertaining Meltdown.

So save outer space for after the bar exam. Especially during the last two weeks, take care of yourself, both psychologically and physically.

Z's And EV's

In other words, these last two weeks, make sure you get lots of Z's and continue to take Emergency Vacations.

Remind yourself that you've been preparing now for over two months; that you know more than you think you know; and that the end is near.

Try to sleep at least eight hours a night, if not more.

If you find yourself particularly panicked, have the courage to take an Emergency Vacation—go see the latest moronic comedy at the multiplex, take your dog for a long walk somewhere beautiful, attend a symphony, schedule dinner at a restaurant you enjoy with a non-bar-exam-contaminated friend.

Confront head on the tempting fallacy that the more minutes you spend studying, the better your chances of passing the bar.

At this point in the process, getting sleep and staying in good physical and emotional shape is much more important than torturing yourself with the minutiae of, say, endorsements.

Instead of sweating inter-vivos trusts, do your best to keep yourself among the vivos.

Chapter 11: The Last 100 Hours

Welcome To The Twilight Zone

Intrepid bar examinee, do not attempt to adjust your television set. You truly have entered another dimension. The last 100 hours before the bar exam is an experience unlike any other. The intoxicating combination of fatigue, anxiety, and razor-sharp legal knowledge will pull you out of everyday experience and your stuffed brain will feel like a hot air balloon raising you up off the earth into the clouds.

You will find it increasingly difficult to relate to non-bar-exam-taking civilians. The intense heat of July or the frigid snows of February will add a climactically extreme, dream-like atmosphere to this, the final phase of your bar exam preparation journey.

Perhaps you will find yourself able to study without distraction. Perhaps you won't be able to study at all. Either way, all you have to do at this point is maintain your psychological sovereignty and your physical health. Think of how far you've come and how short the road that remains.

A Note About Cramming

Bar Exam Heresy

Bar Exam orthodoxy maintains it's not possible to cram for the bar exam.

"It's a marathon, not a sprint," many say.

And up to this point in this guide, I certainly haven't recommended it.

But truth be told, some do indeed choose to sprint. And they do so successfully.

But It's Not Going To Be Pretty

But don't book a Caribbean Vacation for the month of June (or January) just quite yet. As I emphasized above, I recommend attending all lectures (or watching them online), filling out the handouts, and condensing as much of your notes as you can.

Even with all this done, cramming for the bar is not a pleasant experience. But if you were the type who pulled "all-nighters" routinely in college and law school, still writing your papers as the first bird call announced the dawn of the day they were due, then cramming may work for you.

But again, I really don't encourage it.

I certainly wouldn't go into the bar exam preparation experience with the plan of cramming at the end.

But if you find yourself with only days before the exam and aren't even remotely prepared, you might as well give it a try.

How should you cram? If you've managed a Final Review Document, then simply read it as many times as you possibly can, as late into the evening as you can handle.

If you haven't condensed your notes, use the BarBri handouts, or the materials from other prep courses, visually editing as I described above. Don't get bogged down in hypos or details—try to pick up the gist of things and move on.

Walking Away

Okay. The Bar Exam is four or less days away. You look at the tower of notes and handouts on your desk. You look at the pile of BarBri books, as shiny and untouched as the day you got them. You've only condensed your notes for a few of the Multistate subjects. And then there's the matter of those Wills lectures you missed and have been meaning to watch online. And that day of Property.

The legal topics you know nothing about flash nightmarishly through your mind: Future Interests, Inter-Vivos Trusts, The Rights of Trespassers, RAP, the Anti-Lapse Statute, Third Party Beneficiary Contracts, all of Commercial Paper.

You try to look at the situation objectively. It's time to stop fooling yourself, you say. You haven't a chance of passing.

Why go through it at all, you wonder. You visualize the stress of the test center, the Multistate, the local essays. Your stomach churns. And then, just for a moment, you imagine letting go. You won't take it. You feel an enormous weight lifting from your shoulders.

Three words of advice for you should you reach this point: Just Take It. Even if you spend the remainder of your available study time watching Comedy Central, Just Take It. Even if you feel absolutely certain that you will fail, Just Take It.

Why? Because there is no compelling reason not to. Re-conceptualize your sitting for the exam days as a trial run if you have to. Why not go and just see what it's like? You must be at least slightly curious at this point to experience the exam you've heard so much about for years.

But what about the shame of failure, you ask. What about telling people you failed? There's not much difference between telling people you've walked away and telling people you failed. And, there's the biggest reason of all not to withdraw: You just might surprise yourself and pass.

If you're contemplating withdrawal, chances are you're an intelligent person who makes honest self-assessments at critical times. That kind of smart person would make a good lawyer. And that kind of person just might pass the bar exam with less preparation than others.

Sometimes, of course, life can give you no choice. If emergency personal or family situations arise and you can't sit for the exam, make sure to call your state's Board of Bar Examiners to officially withdraw. Otherwise, you will be marked as a no-show, and certain jurisdictions, including NY, are now requiring letters of explanation after two failures to appear at the exam. If you call and officially withdraw before the exam date, you'll be okay.

The Final 10 Hours: Good Night, Sweet Prince(ss)

Whether you've been nerding out for the full ten weeks or cramming for the last couple days, it's crucial to get a full night's rest the evening before the first day of your exam.

Although this may seem like fairly obvious advice from afar, in the Twilight Zone of the final hours sometimes rationality fades in the face of a final rush of panic. You may find yourself reasoning that it's better to read your Secured Transactions outline a few more times so that you'll be prepared should that topic appear on one of the local essays. Besides, you may think, you won't be able to sleep anyway, so you might as well put that time to good use studying.

Don't do it. The night before the Massachusetts exam, I didn't get much sleep. I arrived at the test center in a fog and during the first hour or so of the Multistate I felt slow and cotton-headed. This is what led me to get way off the pace of my game plan and necessitated rushing through the final thirty questions.

Even if you're certain you'll toss and turn for the majority of the evening, get into bed, alone or with a loved one or furry friend, turn out the lights, close your eyes, and do your best to shut down your brain.

Sweet dreams.

Chapter 12: The Two Test Days

Noble, fatigued bar examinee, this is what you've been working towards for upwards of two months. It's game day. What follows are specific recommendations about how to manage the examination days.

Why Are Those Examinees Studying Feverishly At The Test Site?

One of the first things you'll notice when you arrive at the test center is your fellow examinees acting in one of two ways. Roughly half of them will be talking loudly with groups of friends, drinking coffee and managing a remarkable conviviality under the dire circumstances. The other half will be studying, alone, from Conviser, from their own notes, or from Nerd Hall Of Fame laminated self-study charts. Since no jurisdiction's security policy permits bringing study materials of any kind into the test center, these last minute scholars will be lingering at the threshold of the test site, cramming away.

So which approach should you take? I think this depends upon your Game Plan, whether or not you're an examinee who's spitting in the face of received wisdom and attempting to cram for the bar, and your own personal style.

Both approaches have positives and negatives. If you've prepared yourself well, both mentally and psychologically, arriving at the test site centered and calm, free of notes, is an excellent way to greet the Bar Examiners.

But if bringing your notes and studying until the last minute relaxes you, by all means go ahead and geek out. There's always the chance that something you review just before the exam will appear a few minutes later on the exam itself, and you will thank your lucky stars you did this last minute review.

Notes: What To Do With Them?

Okay. So you've decided after reading the above that you would like to try studying at the test site, both immediately prior to the morning session and during the lunch break.

Problem is, all jurisdictions forbid bringing notes of any kind past the security checkpoints leading into the examination.

When I took the summer Massachusetts bar in Boston at the World Trade Center, I brought my condensed Contracts and Property outlines with me to the first day of the exam (which, in MA, is the MBE day).

Since I couldn't bring the notes into the test room, I didn't quite know what to do with them.

In a moment of desperation, I left them with a friendly employee at a Dunkin Donuts adjacent to the test center.

Unfortunately, when I went to retrieve my notes after the exam, this employee was off shift and no one knew where my notes had gone. Ultimately, someone found my property outline in the manager's office. But my Contracts outline had apparently slipped through a donut hole into another dimension, never to be seen or heard from again.

The next day (which, in MA, is the local essay day), I brought a bushel of BarBri FinePoints with me, as well as my condensed notes for the local topics. Just before the morning session, I left my notes with friendly employees at a flower shop inside the Convention Center. During the lunch break, I picked up my notes and reviewed them a as I strolled along Boston Harbor. On my way to the afternoon session, I dropped my notes off at the flower shop again. Not only did the friendly employees wish me luck, they held onto my notes so I could pick them up after the exam had finished.

When I took the NY Bar in Albany during the winter, I didn't bring any notes with me. But I did see many examinees storing their notes with their coats and bags in the coat check. Some had trouble retrieving them during the break because of extremely long coat check lines. (See below for more on coat checks.)

Ultimately, I'd recommend leaving your notes with trustworthy employees at retail establishments at the test center site. But be sure not to leave your *only* copy of your notes, in case they disappear to Munchkin Land to join my Contracts outline.

Insecurity

Before arriving at the test center, review the security policy of your particular jurisdiction. Bar Examiners across the country are increasingly freaked out by the possibilities of electronic cheating. The security policies they write tend to be maddeningly vague. I recommend that whenever you find an element of a security policy unclear, err on the side of caution. The last thing you need on test day is an argument with a proctor staffing the entry points of the test center. Save your persuasive wizardry for the exam itself. What follows are some general recommendations.

- E.T. will NOT be iPhoning home: leave your cell phone at home or in your car or hotel room. Many jurisdictions threaten severe penalties from disciplinary charges to beheading for bringing cell phones into the exam, even if they're turned off.

- You're not Moses: leave your iPad and any other tablets at home. Again, the Bar Examiners and proctors are highly suspicious of any and all electronic devices. Even if you have a Master's Degree in computer science and can demonstrate that there's absolutely no conceivable way you could cheat using your tablet, leave it at home.
- If your jurisdiction permits it, bring a simplified timepiece: in other words, this is not the time to impress your fellow examinees with your retro-cool Casio calculator watch. Not only will the proctors at the security checkpoint not find it retro

or cool, they'll confiscate it and you'll be left without a watch of any kind, a serious disadvantage.

- Hoodwinked: most jurisdictions prohibit "hoodies" and sweats with marsupial pockets. Again, err on the side of over-caution here and don't confuse the bar examination with a social event where you strut your unique brand of urban hip.

Location Scout

Before the first examination day, take an hour or two out from studying to visit the actual site where you'll be sitting for the test. Time how long it takes you to get from your home or hotel to the test site. Scout out places where you can get food during the lunch break, and, if there aren't any restaurants or take-out counters acceptable to you, make plans to bring your own food. (In certain states you can bring food with you into the exam, but can't it eat in the room. In others, you can't even bring food with you into the exam room.)

The purpose here is to control in advance all the factors you can control so there are no stressful surprises on exam days except for, say, an entire essay question devoted to the minutiae of Secured Transactions.

Beware Ronald McDonald

It was the second day of the New York Bar in Albany. MBE day. As I waited for the proctor assigned to my row to collect my answer sheet from this, the morning session, my belly grumbled. I was starving.

I bolted out of the examination room and ran to the McDonald's at the far end of the convention center.

I was one of the first examinees in line, ahead of the giant crush of people I'd witnessed the previous day.

So thrilled to have beaten the crowds, so enthusiastic that I just had one more three-hour testing session to go before being done, and so hungry, I proceeded to order so much food that within minutes my tray was covered in a mountain of paper-wrapped delicacies. There was a Double Quarter Pounder with cheese. A large order of Chicken Selects. A Super-Sized order of fries. A Super-Sized Coke. A giant coffee with cream and sugar. Five satchels of ketchup. Two tubs of barbecue sauce. Two tubs of sweet and sour sauce.

I ran to a table and consumed everything on the tray within fifteen minutes. Admittedly, it was delicious and satisfying, the way I imagine Harold and Kumar felt as they consumed their White Castle meal at the finale of their movie *Harold and Kumar Go To White Castle*.

But when I returned to the examination room and started to work my way through the afternoon session of the MBE, I was way off game. I couldn't concentrate. I read questions two, three, four times and nothing stuck. I felt floaty and out of it.

Then it hit me: Food Coma! I saw Ronald McDonald's giggling face in my mind's eye. After a huge investment of time, money, and energy in bar preparation, I was to be torpedoed by a Double Quarter Pounder with cheese!

Although I ultimately recovered, my foolish lunchtime choices cost me at least 15 minutes of exam time.

I encourage you to make better food choices than I did so you're not Hamburgled out of a passing score on the exam.

February Examinees: Beware The Coat Check Line

When I sat for the New York bar in Albany in February, it was 3 degrees Fahrenheit on the first day of the exam, exclusive of wind chill. I bundled myself up appropriately and headed to the Empire State Plaza.

When I arrived, the first thing I noticed was a long, serpentine line stretching from some mysterious location all the way into the main corridor of the convention center.

What on earth was this? Were examinees so eager to get into the test center they were lining up early? Or was this some other line completely unrelated to the Bar Exam? Were the Rolling Stones making a comeback tour and spending a few nights in rockin' Albany, NY, and this is where the diehard fans were lining up for tickets?

I scanned the people in the line more closely. Definitely not Stones fans. Then I started to notice the telltale BarBri outlines. And clear plastic one gallon Ziploc baggies stuffed with pens. Bar examinees for sure.

After several inquiries, I realized that this was the coat check line. And that I would have to wait in it. Luckily, I had arrived with more than enough time to spare. Even still, I spent at least 30 minutes in line to check my coat. The attendants seemed overwhelmed. If I'd brought my notes and planned to check them along with my coat (say, in a back-pack), I'd have to wait in this line twice during lunch break—once to retrieve my notes, and another time to return them. Little time for lunch or a break.

Thus I warn all February examinees in cold locations to leave an extra amount of time for the coat check line. Better yet, leave your coat at home or in your car or hotel room if at all possible. Even if you have to run for a few frigid seconds through the cold from the parking lot to the test center, you'll save yourself time and a hassle.

To Laptop, Or Not To Laptop

Jurisdictions are increasingly offering examinees the opportunity to use laptops on the local essay day. As you determine whether or not to MacBook the bar, keep the following negatives and positives in mind.

Negatives:

- Additional cost: In most jurisdictions that offer laptop programs, there's an additional fee.
- Software installation: In all jurisdictions, laptop users must install software on their

computers that disables the ability to cheat by preventing any other software from opening during the exam.

- Typing room: Those who use laptops are assigned to smaller, laptop only rooms; if you are easily distracted by noise, weigh the benefits of using your laptop against the very real possibility that you'll find the cacophony of keystrokes irritating.
- Seconds from disaster: Relying on technology is always a risk; using your laptop puts you one computer glitch away from disaster: a processor failure that causes you to lose your work or otherwise delays your progress during the exam.

Positives:

- Road Runner: For most accomplished typists, using a laptop is considerably more speedy than hand writing.
- Revision provision: Word processing your essay answers allows for much easier editing—for both additions and deletions—than writing your exam in pen.
- Legibility: If you suffer from penmanship indecipherable to your fellow human beings, you should have gone to medical school. But seeing as it's too late for that at this point, typing your exam will ensure that

the Bar Examiners can appreciate the full beauty of your legal prose.

- Used those muscles recently? As society becomes more digitized, handwriting is fast becoming a lost art. You may be surprised how difficult you find it to spend a tense six hours handwriting the essay day.

Hand Writing The Local Day? Which Pens Should You Use?

What a wonderfully old-fashioned choice. I have two major recommendations for you.

First, practice makes perfect. As I mentioned above, we all handwrite a good deal less these days. Before exam day, I recommend practicing handwriting for long stretches of time to simulate the six hours of writing you'll do during the local day.

If you're enrolled in Barbri, a perfect opportunity for this kind of practice is taking notes in longhand for the few bar prep lectures that don't use handouts. You'll find that after a day or two of taking lecture notes for three to four hours a day, you'll begin to get back into the swing of the ancient craft of longhand, middle finger callus and all.

Second, I'd recommend finding a friendly species of pen. Not only is researching and trying out different pens a fun way to procrastinate, you'll want to have some familiarity with the instruments you'll be relying upon on local day.

I used the Pentel EnerGel RTX Retractable roller ball, medium point. Unfortunately, I am in no way sponsored by Pentel. The EnerGel just fit my hand nicely and wrote very smoothly. They are not the cheapest pens, but why economize on something so essential in the grand scheme of bar prep expenses? Would a surgeon buy a discount scalpel?

I bought two dozen pens and brought about a dozen fresh ones with me on test day. Although these pens are refillable I didn't bother with refills. During the exam, as one ran out of ink, I merely picked up a new one and continued writing.

And for the artistic ones among you, remember that most jurisdictions limit pen colors to blue and black. Bar exam day is not the time to experiment with fuchsia, mauve, and rainbow ink.

Bring Bushels Of Pencils For MBE Day

As I guess is becoming increasingly obvious to you, I'm a bit of a stationery supplies nerd. Some of my Emergency Vacations during bar exam prep consisted of a drive to the nearest Staples to walk through the aisles.

For MBE day, only number 2 pencils are allowed. No pens. No highlighters. No crayons, quills, charcoal, or spray paint.

Even within this strict limitation, there are dozens of different varieties of pencils to choose from. Are you a traditionalist who will select the sturdy Dixon Ticonderoga? Or are you an artsy type who prefers your black clothes to be matched by the stylish black casing of the Mirado Black Warrior? Maybe you like nothing better than a good bargain and can find a no-name brand online that sells for pennies each. Or maybe you're into convenience and will just make a quick visit to the nearest CVS, Duane Reade, or Wal-Mart and purchase the first number two's you see.

Whichever you choose, I have one important piece of advice: buy a lot of them, and bring a lot of them with you. Like at least 12, if not 20 or 30.

Do I have a brother-in-law in the pencil business? No.

Here's why. The security policies of some jurisdictions prohibit bringing pencil sharpeners of any kind. Bring two pencils and smash two points and you'll suddenly find yourself stressed about a situation you could have avoided by nerding out before hand and bringing enough pencils to build a log cabin. Some test centers may have old-fashioned pencil sharpeners for examinees to use, but why waste the time?

You cannot control what questions will be on the MBE or how difficult they are. What you can control are all the little preparatory factors that, if not paid attention to, could cause you stress during the exam. Bringing enough pencils is one of them. You can also be a bar exam hero by spreading your #2 wealth around to those examinees who showed up with one or two pencils with dull points.

I'd stay away from mechanical pencils. Not only do the security policies of some jurisdictions expressly prohibit them, they could also jam up on you at just the wrong moment, say, when there's ten seconds remaining and you've just erased an MBE answer and want to fill in another "corresponding oval" but can't because your mechanical pencil won't deliver any lead.

Batteries Not Included

Imagine this. You're an hour and a half into the morning session of the Multistate. Things are going pretty well. Sure, you're making lots of educated guesses and aren't certain about as many of your answers as you'd like, but hey, this is the MBE. Most people are getting at least 70 wrong. You know this, and you're motoring on.

As you get to question 55, a seven paragraph mortgage killer with answers referencing legal principles you've never before encountered, you consult your watch, if your jurisdiction permits one.

You're amazed, because you're way ahead of schedule. "I'm kicking butt," you think.

At question 60, a loopy dormant commerce clause question, you check your watch again.

An ice-cold wave of fear crests in your stomach.

Your watch has stopped.

You flick the crystal of your watch with your thumb as if this will magically resuscitate time. Nothing happens.

You scan the convention center room for the nearest clock. For a moment, you can't find any. Around you hundreds of test takers continue blackening corresponding ovals, purposefully turning the pages of their test booklets. You hope you're having a nightmare and will wake up soon.

I'm sure you can continue the scenario.

Of all the things you bring with you on exam days, and if your jurisdiction permits it, a trusty timepiece is by far the most important. Instead of working through the Rule Against Perpetuities one last time, go and get your watch battery changed with a fresh one.

Even if you buy a brand new watch for the exam, you may want to think of replacing that battery. It can be very difficult to gauge how long a watch has sat on a store shelf—and impossible if you got it from Amazon or another online retailer.

You may also want to bring two watches, one as a back-up, if your jurisdiction allows this.

The week after I sat for the NY Bar in February, I put on my watch one day and the battery had gone dead. I realized I had just had a very close call.

In sum, don't let an over $100,000 investment in legal education and thousands more in test prep be tanked by a three dollar battery.

High Noon

An additional watch hint I found helpful. Before each testing session begins, set your analog or digital watch to 12:00pm. That way, you can easily calculate how much time is remaining in a morning or afternoon session.

You'll find that none of the sessions start exactly on the hour or half-hour. So if you keep your watch set to the actual time, you may find it more difficult to calculate how much time has elapsed and how much remains.

You could also try to use the chronograph function of an analog watch or a digital countdown function. Personally, I think these are more trouble than they're worth. Often digital watches can emit unpredictable beeps on such settings, and this could lead to a highly disruptive proctor interaction. Furthermore, some security policies are so vaguely written that they seem to potentially ban using any digital watch features except basic timekeeping. Exam day is not the time to test the security rules, even if they ironically suffer from the Constitutional defects of overbreadth and vagueness.

Confrontation With The Gum Snapper

Finally, during the exam itself, do not let yourself be brought down by other examinees who are engaging in distracting behavior.

During the afternoon session of the MBE in Albany, about 30 minutes after my show-down with Ronald McDonald (as described above), I hit a string of five long, difficult questions in a row. Three of them dealt with complicated mortgage arrangements and the rest were multi-paragraph property monsters complete with exhaustive descriptions of the intergenerational transfer of parcels.

As I tried to work my way through these questions, a noise behind me repeatedly interrupted my thoughts. It was an unpredictable yet relatively frequent snapping sound. I turned and saw the source: the examinee behind me was chewing gum and, after a bit of chewing, repeatedly "snapping" it.

At first I tried to ignore the sound. Now that I knew the source, I hoped that I could filter it out. I resumed reading one of the mortgage questions, and mid-way through, the loud snapping interrupted me. I tried to ignore it again, and again was interrupted.

I then attempted shooting the examinee a variety of death stares.

Didn't work. Either the examinee didn't see me, or did see me and decided it was best to ignore me.

Finally, I couldn't take it anymore. I turned around and said, "Could you please stop snapping your gum?"

I then turned back around and continued the exam. The snapping stopped. In fact, the examinee spit out the gum and stopped chewing it altogether. I got through the stretch of difficult questions and finished the exam.

As we waited for the proctors to pick up our answer sheets, I turned back to the examinee and apologized, explaining that I'd hit a tough stretch of questions. My fellow test-taker was amiable and took the whole thing in stride.

I therefore encourage you to confront test takers around you who are engaged in behavior that threatens your performance.

Obviously you don't want to become the Travis Bickle of your bar exam, yelling willy-nilly at everyone around you. That kind of performance will likely merit some interaction from the proctors.

But if you are enduring a distraction in silence, and you give it some time to subside and it doesn't, a polite confrontation is preferable to seriously compromising your performance on the exam.

You've simply worked too hard and come too far to put up with it.

Chapter 13: After It's Over

If You Think You Failed, You Passed; If You Think You Passed, You Failed

Well okay, maybe it's not that simple.

But rest assured: the vast majority of examinees leave the second day of the bar exam feeling there's a real chance they haven't passed.

I felt this both times. I've already mentioned above my experience falling far behind during the morning session of the MBE. I distinctly remember looking at my watch and calculating that I had 30 minutes or so to complete the final 30 questions—far quicker than my goal pace of roughly two minutes per question. I rushed through those final 30 questions at a frantic pace, skipping entire paragraphs.

Although I managed my time much more effectively during the afternoon session of the MBE, I was haunted by my poor time management in the morning.

In order not to torpedo my performance on the local essay day (which, in MA, follows the Wednesday administration of the Multistate), I reminded myself that most passing candidates in MA were getting at least 70 MBE questions wrong, so that even if I had bombed on every single one of the 30 questions I rushed through, I still had a minimum of 40 others to get wrong while still passing.

The following day, the first essay question of the afternoon local session was Commercial Paper—a topic rarely tested on the MA Bar (thanks, Subject Frequency Chart). I shoveled the legal manure, including legal principles not only never promulgated in MA, but never seen in our solar system. Then, sticking to my game plan, I moved on and completed the remaining essays.

As the proctor announced the end of exam, examinees at the Boston Harbor Convention Center broke into cheers and applause. At the exits from the testing room, friends and relatives of fellow examinees stood holding large poster board signs declaring: Congratulations, You Just Passed The MA Bar Exam!

"I doubt it," I thought to myself as I walked across the Harbor to the subway. The Commercial Paper question and my rush through the last 30 morning Multistate questions haunted me.

As the months progressed, other parts of the exam with which I'd struggled haunted me as well, such as a reference to a type of special conference attorneys can request according to the MA rules of Civil Procedure. Had I identified the right one? Further, should I have written that it could have been a diversity case? Or was there a federal question I'd missed? As my memories of the exam and my responses faded, my doubts increased, feeding on my uncertainties about what I'd written.

When I received my pass letter in October, all of these doubts vanished once and for all.

After the NY Bar, I was haunted by a string of MBE mortgage questions I'd found particularly difficult. As well as by my run-in with Ronald McDonald, discussed above, and my need to confront the Gum Snapper, also discussed above.

As I drove from Albany back to Boston, I torturously thought through some of the Multistate questions. Should I have picked that other answer? How many was it likely I got wrong? Once again, doubts fed upon doubts, and I started to question my performance on the Wills essay. It seemed too easy, and I knew that finding a bar exam essay easy often meant I'd missed a great deal of the law. Was it actually an elective share question in disguise?

When I received my pass letter in May, these doubts vanished too, of course.

In retrospect, what's amazing to me is the universality of this experience. Nearly every bar examinee with whom I spoke—both those who took it with me, before me, and after me—went through the same thing. The specific doubts were different, but the sense of the likelihood of failure the same.

I think the roots of this lay in the scholarly disposition and track record of academic success, if not downright dominance, in the past of most of those attracted to the legal profession. As I've emphasized ad nauseum in this guide, one of the most amazing features of the bar exam in every jurisdiction is the highly mediocre essay scores and Multistate performance of the average passing candidate. Add to this the fact that in most jurisdictions, you can make up a poor performance on one exam day with a better performance on the other, and there's the potential to "bomb" one day and still pass.

What I recommend is that you try to maintain the same kinds of psychological sovereignty post-exam that you did as you prepared for the exam. (This would be a clear case of do as I say and not as I did.) Remember that most examinees feel they failed, have some compassion for yourself, and hope for the best.

Now, what, you ask, if you don't leave the bar exam with doubts about your performance? Does this mean you're doomed to failure?

Of course not. It means that you've done a great job maintaining psychological sovereignty and a positive outlook. You've kept your focus on the big picture and wisely understand that at this point, there's no use agonizing about things you can't change.

Postpartum

Postpartum is a form of depression suffered by nearly a quarter of women (and some of their husbands) upon the birth of their child. The end of nine months of pregnancy is experienced as a tremendous loss and induces sadness.

Although you may find this very hard to believe, the end of the bar exam can engender some of these same feelings in examinees.

To be sure, post-childbirth postpartum is a serious condition that often requires psychiatric treatment.

Post-bar exam postpartum is a milder experience, but an emotional reality for some nonetheless.

Where do these strange feelings come from? Wouldn't one predict just the opposite after the bar exam is over: feelings of liberation, jubilation, and overall well-being?

I locate the source of these strange feelings of loss in the intensity of the ten weeks plus of the bar exam preparation experience. The swelling of the examinee's brain with legal knowledge can be compared to a pregnancy, with delivery occurring during the two examination days.

Suddenly, the day after, there's no outlet for all that hard-earned legal expertise.

Many lawyers say they never possessed more legal knowledge then they did while studying for the bar exam. This makes sense because of the huge breadth of the topics studied for the bar as compared to the specialization of most lawyers' practice.

I remember vividly the sense I had while studying for the bar that, for this limited time, I would know quite a bit about nearly every possible societal interaction, from birth to death, arrest to jail, contract to courtroom.

Despite the understandable anxiety about the exam itself, I think these weeks are heady times for all examinees. Non-lawyers are awed by you and your bar preparation, and you begin to experience the enhanced social status and cachet of being a lawyer. Strangers will ask you for legal advice, interest in your online dating profile will surge, and friends and family will start bragging about you.

Suddenly, after the bar exam, the intensity of the experience turns off. The legal knowledge starts to fade away while fears of not passing take their place.

In a sense, post-bar, you return to civilian life on planet earth and enter the purgatory of waiting to pass in order to obtain your license to practice.

Something has indeed been lost—the intense high of integrating vast amounts of legal knowledge, and the feeling of power that can accompany it.

The good news is that post-bar postpartum tends to pass relatively quickly. If you've arranged a post-bar trip, a few days on the beach will cure you. Even if you haven't, within a few weeks you not only won't miss the bar exam experience, you'll be deeply grateful that it's over and you survived it, morning sickness and all.

Results, Or, Waiting For Godot

Part of the peculiar cruelty of the bar exam in every jurisdiction is the long wait between sitting for the exam and receiving results.

In most states the wait is around three months, give or take a few weeks.

After the summer Massachusetts bar, I found that after a month or so I didn't think about the bar or the results all that much.

Until right around Halloween. That's when I read online, on sites like Above The Law, rumors that the Commonwealth had sent out the results. They were to arrive the following Monday in the mail.

I approached my mailbox that Monday evening with a trepidation I hadn't experienced since I awaited decision letters from colleges my senior year in high school. My heart rate spiked as I opened it and flipped through the contents: a credit card bill, an electric bill, a copy of The New Yorker, and a thin envelope without a return address marked "Urgent: Open Immediately." My hands shaking, I tore open the letter marked urgent and unfolded the thick piece of paper inside.

"Entertainment Weekly wants you back!" it declared in big letters. "Special discount rate for former subscribers expires November 15th."

If you can resist the temptation to follow each new rumor, you'll avoid receiving the periodical industry award for most intense read of an Entertainment Weekly subscription offer.

Chapter 14: If You Need To Take It Again

We Regret To Inform You . . .

This was not the letter or e-mail you were hoping for. As you read and re-read it, the reality sinks in: You're going to have to go through the whole bar exam preparation and test taking experience again.

You should have gone to medical school, you scold yourself. Or moved to the South of France to become a painter. You see yourself in a black beret drinking from a jug of wine as you stand before a canvas in a field of dandelions.

As days turn into weeks, the understandable emotional experience of sadness, frustration, and anger ebbs. You never were one for Organic Chemistry. Nor do you really want to cut off your ear in a fit of pique and FedEx it to your beloved.

You turn your attention to preparing, once again, for the next administration of the bar exam.

On The Bright Side

While no one wants to repeat the bar exam preparation experience, there are some distinct advantages you'll enjoy the second time around.

Freebie

BarBri and most other prep courses allow you to repeat the course for the jurisdiction in which you were unsuccessful for free. This is usually limited to the very next administration of the course.

Detailed Exam Results

In most states, successful candidates receive very little information about their performance on specific parts of the bar exam. In Massachusetts, passers receive no information at all about their scores. In New York, successful test takers only receive their Multistate score.

Unsuccessful candidates, on the other hand, receive detailed score reports in many jurisdictions. Information about your performance on specific local day essay questions is quite valuable. As you prepare for the next administration of the exam, you can use this detailed feedback as a guide to what you need to emphasize in your study plan.

You've Experienced The Unknown

One of the biggest challenges facing examinees is the tremendous amount of anxiety created by the myths and rumors surrounding the bar exam. While this guide attempts to chip away at these understandable fears, nothing beats actually experiencing the bar exam yourself.

Repeaters have already gone through the experience and know what to expect. The peculiarities of the particular test center you'll attend, the strange behavior of your fellow examinees, the best strategy for lunch—you've already experienced these elements and won't be psyched out by any of them.

This is a tremendous advantage repeaters have over first timers.

You Already Have Your Holy Grail

Another huge advantage to being a repeat taker is that you've already condensed your notes into some sort of Final Review Document.

Maybe you never got a chance to finish. Maybe your notes were overly condensed, or far too detailed.

Whatever the case, you have some significant work product that first time test takers don't.

It may need to be revised, tweaked, and polished, but it exists.

This puts you way ahead of the game.

Groundhog Day

And so it begins again. Like Bill Murray's character in the movie *Groundhog Day*, you'll feel as if life has become nightmarishly familiar.

Here, again, you'll be sitting in a BarBri class with a largely new crop of examinees. Although the faces will have changed, the character types will not. There will be the self-anointed experts talking loudly about their practice question scores and the nervous quiet huddled masses.

But you will have a secret. You've been here before. You know the louder the examinee pontificates, the less they know.

What's more, again like Bill Murray's weatherman, you'll often know what the lecturer is about to say, because you've seen these lectures before.

That leads to one of the biggest decisions you'll have as a repeater. Even though the course is free, should you attend all the lectures again?

I'd say you should definitely watch the lectures for any topics you missed the first time around.

Next, it would probably be a good idea to re-watch the lectures for the subjects you did most poorly on during the exam. Use the detailed results your jurisdiction provided you with as a guide.

Also, if the first time around you had a particularly negative transference reaction to a lecturer, and that reaction inhibited your ability to master that subject, you may want to try that lecturer again, doing your best to ignore the personality quirks you find irritating and focus on the law.

Although you'll find that most of the lecturers and actual lectures will be the same (unless you're at the live location this time), there are usually at least one or two changes. If a professor you had a hard time with has been replaced with someone new, definitely try out that new lecturer to determine if their explanation of the law works better for you.

From the very beginning this time, work on your Holy Grail from last time. As I emphasized above, not having to start from scratch is a huge advantage.

Finally, just as your detailed score report can guide you in which legal topics to emphasize, give yourself a psychological score report on how you managed the entire preparation and examination experience the last time around. Didn't get enough sleep the last week? This time, resolve to get ten hours a night for the last two weeks. Stressed out so much last time that you took the exam with a brewing case of influenza? This time, use as many relaxation techniques as you can think of to keep yourself calm.

In other words, leverage the biggest advantage you've been given by the opportunity to re-take the exam: learning from your past mistakes.

You're In Good Company

One other thing. Hilary Clinton. Jerry Brown. Kathleen Sullivan. Ed Koch. Elizabeth Wurtzel. Michelle Obama. Franklin D. Roosevelt. Benjamin Cardozo.

All of them failed the bar exam at least once.

So you're definitely in good company.

Chapter 15: Concluding Thoughts

Surely one would have to be demented to enjoy the grueling and somewhat absurd experience of bar exam preparation and examination.

But as I've pointed out repeatedly, this doesn't have to be the worst summer or winter of your life.

Overall, there are three components to this experience: psychological, mental, and physical.

On the psychological level, do your best to maintain emotional sovereignty. Treat yourself to emergency vacations when you feel yourself starting to drag. Keep one eye on the larger picture at all times.

On the mental level, condensing your notes into a Final Review Document is paramount. This will be the Holy Grail you cherish like a monk clutching a precious manuscript during the Dark Ages.

And on the physical level, don't let yourself get so worn down you get sick. Get plenty of sleep, eat well, and de-stress often.

You are on the threshold of joining one of the noblest professions in the history of mankind. I wish you not only the best of luck on the bar exam, but throughout what I hope will be a robust, challenging, and rewarding career.

Made in the USA
Monee, IL
05 November 2026

67806908R00154